YALE LANGUAGE SERIES

D1613865

今日汉语会话 Speaking Chinese in China

HSU YING 徐英

J. MARVIN BROWN

YALE UNIVERSITY PRESS
NEW HAVEN AND LONDON

Printed in the United States of America by
The Murray Printing Co., Westford, Massachusetts.

Pictures by Lin Wancui 林琬崔
and Zhang Lewa 张 乐娃

Tapes to accompany *Speaking Chinese in China*
are available from Audio-Forum, a division of
Jeffrey Norton Publishers, Inc., On The Green,
Guilford, Connecticut 06437.

Library of Congress Catalog Card Number: 85–40010

ISBN 0-300-02955-1
IBSN 0-300-03032-0 (pbk.)

10   9   8   7   6   5   4

CONTENTS

目录

PREFACE

This book has two main purposes. 1) It is intended to be used as a *second-year conversation course* that can follow *any* first-year course in Mandarin Chinese; and 2) it is intended to prepare the students to use their Chinese in *China*. These two points are explained below.

1. This book focuses on *using* sentences—not making them. It is assumed here that a feeling for how sentences are put together (their internal grammar) must be rendered largely to the unconscious before the student can keep his attention on how these sentences are used in situations (their external 'grammar'). *Making* sentences is thus first-year business; *using* them, second. This doesn't mean that using sentences is not a good teaching technique in a first-year course; it may, in fact, be one of the best. It simply means that in actual fact we can expect better results in making sentences in a first-year course; and if we get these results, we can then expect excellent results in using sentences in a second-year course. So if some of the topics of the lessons in this book seem to be identical with those in most first-year courses, it should be remembered that the expected results in using these topics are quite different.

2. Since travel to China by people from English-speaking countries was restricted for nearly thirty years, Chinese text-books written in English tended to specialize in Chinese used outside of China. But now, with the opening up of China, there is a need for using Chinese *inside* China, and many students will be starting with a variety of Chinese that isn't quite right for their purposes. This is not a serious problem, since the differences between the Mandarin Chinese used inside and outside of China are not big. These differences consist of 1) the use of simplified characters in China, 2) the use of the pinyin transcription in China, and 3) minor differences in usage and culture. This book leads the student from any non-China-oriented course toward all three differences. But it isn't exclusively for the use of such students. Those from China-oriented courses can also profitably use this book: either as a natural continuation of their goal to use Chinese in China, or, in reverse, to learn the full characters and Yale transcription.

INTRODUCTION

Format and Use

This book consists of twenty lessons, and each lesson has four main parts.

1. The main dialog (sections A-F)
2. Substitutions (sections G-H)
3. Mini dialogs (sections I-J)
4. Cultural notes (section K)

The **main dialog** serves to introduce vocabulary and patterns needed for the topic of the lesson.

The **substitutions** serve mainly to introduce additional vocabulary that fits the patterns of the main dialog and to drill new patterns that occur in the dialog.

The **mini dialogs** sometimes introduce additional vocabulary, but their main purpose is to lead the student from fixed dialogs to spontaneous speaking. The following three steps show one way of doing this. 1) The student memorizes mini dialogs and practices them up to fluent speed. 2) The teacher makes slight modifications as she shoots rapid questions from student to student. 3) The teacher departs more and more from the mini dialogs and leads the students to spontaneous speaking within the topic of the lesson.

The **cultural notes** are a small but important part of each lesson. They appear at the end of the lesson, but should probably be read first.

The main dialog of each lesson is arranged on three sets of facing pages as shown below.

A	B		C	D		E	F
Pinyin transcription	Simplified characters		Yale transcription	Full characters		Vocabulary and notes	English

With at most a flip of a page and a glance at the same place on the new page, any cross reference can readily be made. The purpose of this rather elaborate arrangement is to get the student to read pages A and B by giving him the necessary help from pages C, D, E, and F.

The substitutions and the mini dialogs are arranged in such a way that the student can see the vocabulary and four versions of everything without turning a page, as shown below.

G or I	H or J
Full characters	Simplified characters
English	Pinyin
Vocabulary	

This gives the student most of the help he needs but forces him to dispense with the Yale transcription. And all vocabulary entries force him to dispense with the full characters as well.

Transcription Conventions

Two different conventions are used for showing weak (tone-less) syllables, as seen in the following examples: dōng∙xī (the raised dot means that the following syllable is toneless) and dōngxi (the lack of a tone marker shows that the syllable is toneless). The former convention is used mainly for learning new words (in vocabulary lists and substitution drills), where the student needs to be told what tone has been lost. The latter convention is used mostly in dialogs, where the student already knows the word's original tone and just needs reminding that the syllable is weak and thus toneless.

No rigid policy is followed in deciding which syllables should be written weak and which syllables should be joined together into a single word. The same expression, in fact, might be written differently in different places. Decisions are made separately for each instance on the basis of what seems to be most helpful to the student for that particular case. When the joining together of two syllables to form a single word leads to a glaring ambiguity, a hyphen is used (notice that píngān could be read either píng-ān or pín-gān).

Correspondences between the Yale and Pinyin Transcriptions

Students whose first-year course used the Yale transcription should make the effort to learn the pinyin transcription while studying from this book. Correspondence tables for problem sounds are given below in an arrangement that points up the systematic aspects of the correspondences. The first line establishes the pattern. The boxes that don't have internal lines add nothing to the original pattern, but are given to help point up comparisons.

Pin	zi	ci	si		zhi	chi	shi		ji	qi	xi
Yale	dz	tsz	sz		jr	chr	shr		ji	chi	syi

Pin	zu	cu	su		zhu	chu	shu		ju	qu	xu
Yale	dzu	tsu	su		ju	chu	shu		jyu	chyu	syu

Pin	ze	ce	se		zhe	che	she		jie	qie	xie
Yale	dze	tse	se		je	che	she		jye	chye	sye

Pin	zuo	cuo	suo		zhuo	chuo	shuo		jue	que	xue
Yale	dzwo	tswo	swo		jwo	chwo	shwo		jywe	chywe	sywe

Pin	za	ca	sa		zha	cha	sha		jia	qia	xia
Yale	dza	tsa	sa		ja	cha	sha		jya	chya	sya

Pin	zuan	cuan	suan		zhuan	chuan	shuan		juan	quan	xuan
Yale	dzwan	tswan	swan		jwan	chwan	shwan		jywan	chywan	sywan

Pin	-iu	-ui		-ao	-ong		(n,l) ü	(n,l) üe		(b,p,m,f) o
Yale	-you	-wei		-au	-ung		(n,l) yu	(n,l)ywe		(b,p,m,f)wo

Correspondences between the Wade-Giles and Pinyin Transcriptions

Students whose first-year course used the Wade-Giles transcription should make the effort to learn the pinyin transcription while studying from this book. Correspondence tables are given below in an arrangement that points up the systematic aspects of the correspondences.

Pin	b, p	d, t	g, k	z, c	zh, ch, r	j, q, x
W-G	p, p'	t, t'	k, k'	ts, ts'	ch, ch', j	ch, ch', hs

Pin	er	yi	you	-ong	ye, -ie	yan, -ian	(g, k) ui
W-G	erh	i	yu	-ung	yeh, -ieh	yen, -ien	(k, k') uei

Pin	(j, q, x, y) u, ue	zi ci si	(zh, ch, sh, r) i
W-G	(ch, ch', hs, y) ü, üeh	tzu tz'u szu	(ch, ch', sh, j) ih

Pin	(g, k, h) e, e, uo	(z, c, s, zh, ch, d, t, r, l, n) uo
W-G	(k, k', h) e, o, uo	(ts, ts', s, ch, ch', t, t', j, l, n) o

Simplified Characters

About 2,000 of the 5,000 most commonly used characters have simplified forms. But the task of learning the simplified forms for characters you already know is not as big as you might think since a big majority of them are accounted for by only a few dozen character components (radicals and phonetics). The following seven simplified radical forms, in fact, account for over one-third of all simplified characters.

Full form	貝	糸	言	金	門	食	馬
Simplified form	贝	纟	讠	钅	门	饣	马

LESSON 1

INTRODUCING PEOPLE

介 绍 别 人

A. Dialog: Pinyin Transcription

Wáng:	Àiméi, zhèi wèi shì Gélín xiānsheng,	1
	zhèi wèi shì Gélín tàitai.	2
	Tāmen gāng cóng Měiguo lái.	3
	Zhèi shì wǒ àirén, Mǎ Àiméi.	4
Gélín xiānsheng:	Nǐ hǎo.	5
Àiméi:	Nǐ hǎo.	6
Wáng:	Gélín xiānsheng hé tāde tàitai	7
	hěn xiǎng kànkan Zhōngguo de jiātíng,	8
	suǒyǐ wǒ qǐng tāmen lái wǒmen jiā le.	9
Àiméi:	Ò, huānyíng, huānyíng.	10
Wáng:	Zhèi shì wǒ nǚér, Wáng Lìli,	11
	zhōngxuésheng.	12
Lìli:	Nǐ hǎo.	13
Gélín xiānsheng:	Nǐ hǎo.	14
Wáng:	Wǒ érzi zài dàxué lǐ xuéxi,	15
	bú zài jiā.	16
	Dàjiā qǐng zuò a, qǐng hē chá ba.	17

B. Dialog: Simplified Characters

王：	爱梅，这位是格林先生，	1
	这位是格林太太。	2
	他们刚从美国来。	3
	这是我爱人、马爱梅。	4
格林先生：	你好。	5
爱梅：	你好。	6
王：	格林先生和他的太太	7
	很想看看中国的家庭，	8
	所以我请他们来我们家了。	9
爱梅：	喔，欢迎，欢迎。	10
王：	这是我女儿王丽丽、	11
	中学生。	12
丽丽：	你好。	13
格林先生：	你好。	14
王：	我儿子在大学里学习，	15
	不在家。	16
	大家请坐啊，请喝茶吧。	17

C. Dialog: Yale Transcription

Wáng:	Àiméi, jèi wèi shr̀ Gélín syānsheng,	1
	jèi wèi shr̀ Gélín tàitai.	2
	Tāmen gāng tsúng Měigwo lái.	3
	Jèi shr̀ wǒ àirén, Mǎ Àiméi.	4
Gélín syānsheng:	Nǐ hǎu.	5
Àiméi:	Nǐ hǎu.	6
Wáng:	Gélín syānsheng hé tāde tàitai	7
	hěn syǎng kànkan Jūnggwo de jyātíng,	8
	swǒyǐ wǒ chǐng tāmen lái wǒmen jyā le.	9
Àiméi:	Ò, hwānyíng, hwānyíng.	10
Wáng:	Jèi shr̀ wǒ nyǔér, Wáng Lìli,	11
	jūngsywésheng.	12
Lìli:	Nǐ hǎu.	13
Gélín syānsheng:	Nǐ hǎu.	14
Wáng:	Wǒ érdz dzài dàsywé lǐ sywésyi,	15
	bú dzài jyā.	16
	Dàjyā chǐng dzwò a, chǐng hē chá ba.	17

D. DIALOG: FULL CHARACTERS

王：　　　　愛梅，這位是格林先生，　　　　　1
　　　　　　這位是格林太太。　　　　　　　　　2
　　　　　　他們剛從美國來。　　　　　　　　　3
　　　　　　這是我愛人、馬愛梅。　　　　　　　4

格林先生：　你好。　　　　　　　　　　　　　　5

愛梅：　　　你好。　　　　　　　　　　　　　　6

王：　　　　格林先生和他的太太　　　　　　　　7
　　　　　　很想看看中國的家庭，　　　　　　　8
　　　　　　所以我請他們來我們家了。　　　　　9

愛梅：　　　喔，歡迎，歡迎。　　　　　　　　　10

王：　　　　這是我女兒王麗麗、　　　　　　　　11
　　　　　　中學生。　　　　　　　　　　　　　12

麗麗：　　　你好。　　　　　　　　　　　　　　13

格林先生：　你好。　　　　　　　　　　　　　　14

王：　　　　我兒子在大學裏學習，　　　　　　　15
　　　　　　不在家。　　　　　　　　　　　　　16
　　　　　　大家請坐啊，請喝茶吧。　　　　　　17

E. DIALOG: VOCABULARY AND NOTES.

Situation. Tom Green, an English teacher at Northern University in China, told his Chinese colleague, Professor Wang, that he would like to visit a Chinese family. So Professor Wang takes Mr. and Mrs. Green to his own home and introduces them to his family.

介绍	jièshào To introduce.	家庭	jiātíng Family.
别人	bié rén Other people.	欢迎	huānyíng To welcome.
位	wèi Respectful classifier for people.	中学	zhōngxué High school, middle school.
刚	gāng Just, just now.	中学生	zhōngxué∘shēng A high school student.
爱人	ài rén Husband or wife.	学习	xué∘xí To study.
想	xiǎng To think of (doing); thus, 'to want (to do)'.	大家	dàjiā Everybody.
		喝茶	hē chá To drink tea.

F. Dialog: English

Wang:	Aimei, this is Mr. Green.	1
	And this is Mrs. Green.	2
	They've just come from America.	3
	This is my wife, Ma Aimei.	4
Mr. Green:	How are you?	5
Aimei:	Fine thanks. How are you?	6
Wang:	Mr. Green and his wife	7
	wanted very much to see a Chinese family,	8
	so I invited them to come to our house.	9
Aimei:	Oh, welcome!	10
Wang:	This is my daughter, Wang Lili.	11
	She's a high school student.	12
Lili:	Hi.	13
Mr. Green:	Hi.	14
Wang:	My son is studying at the university,	15
	so he isn't at home now.	16
	Please sit down, everybody, and have some tea.	17

G. SUBSTITUTIONS: FULL CHARACTERS AND ENGLISH

1. 這是我女兒.   丈夫   兒子
    妹妹   姐姐   母親
    愛人   父親   太太
    弟弟   哥哥   朋友

    This is my daughter.   husband   son
             younger sister older sister   mother
             husband or wife father   wife
             younger brother older brother   friend

2. 愛梅,   這位是   格林先生.
    王醫生   老王
    馬教授   格林太太
    小王   林醫生
    格林小姐   李太平
    老林   王教授

    Aimei,   this is   Mr. Green.
    Dr. Wang   'Old Wang'
    Professor Ma   Mrs. Green
    'Little Wang'   Dr. Lin
    Miss Green   Li Taiping
    'Old Lin'   Professor Wang

医生   yī·shēng
       Doctor.

教授   jiàoshòu
       Professor.

1. 介绍 别人   9

H. SUBSTITUTIONS: SIMPLIFIED CHARACTERS AND PINYIN

1.

这是我女儿.	丈夫	儿子
妹妹	姐姐	母亲
爱人	父亲	太太
弟弟	哥哥	朋友

Zhèi shì wǒ nǚér.　　　zhàng‧fū　　　　ér‧zǐ
　　　mèimei　　　　　jiějie　　　　　mǔ‧qīn
　　　àirén　　　　　　fù‧qīn　　　　　tàitai
　　　dìdi　　　　　　gēge　　　　　　péng‧yǒu

2.

爱梅，这位是	格林先生.
王医生	老王
马教授	格林太太
小王	林医生
格林小姐	李太平
老林	王教授

Àiméi,　　　zhèi wèi shì　　Gélín xiān‧shēng.
Wáng yī‧shēng　　　　　　Lǎo Wáng
Mǎ jiàoshòu　　　　　　　Gélín tàitai
Xiǎo Wáng　　　　　　　　Lín yī‧shēng
Gélín xiǎojiě　　　　　　Lǐ Tàipíng
Lǎo Lín　　　　　　　　　Wáng jiàoshòu

小姐　xiǎojě
　　　Miss.

G (2)

3.

王麗麗，	中學生.
老馬	北海大學的教授
馬愛梅	這個醫院的醫生
小王	大學生
王平	北方大學的教授
李太平	兒童醫院的醫生

Wang Lili,	a high school student.
'Old Ma'	a professor at Beihai University
Ma Aimei	a doctor at this hospital
'Little Wang'	a university student
Wang Ping	a professor at Northern University
Li Taiping	a doctor at the Children's Hospital

4.

我兒子，	在北海大學學習.
老李	在中國大學教中文
王醫生	在這個醫院工作
我妹妹	在這個中學學習
李女士	在這兒工作

My son	studies at Beihai University.
'Old Li'	teaches Chinese at the University of China
Dr. Wang	works at this hospital
My younger sister	studies at this high school
Ms. Li	works here

医院 yīyuàn
Hospital.

儿童 értóng
Children.

H (2)

3.

王丽丽,	中学生.
老马	北海大学的教授
马爱梅	这个医院的医生
小王	大学生
王平	北方大学的教授
李太平	儿童医院的医生

Wáng Lìli,	zhōngxué·shēng.
Lǎo Mǎ	Běihǎi dàxué de jiàoshòu
Mǎ Àiméi	zhèige yīyuàn de yī·shēng
Xiǎo Wáng	dàxué·shēng
Wáng Píng	Běifāng dàxué de jiàoshòu
Lǐ Tàipíng	értóng yīyuàn de yī·shēng

4.

我儿子,	在北海大学学习.
老李	在中国大学教中文
王医生	在这个医院工作
我妹妹	在这个中学学习
李女士	在这儿工作

Wǒ ér·zi	zài Běihǎi dàxué xué·xí.
Lǎo Lǐ	zài Zhōngguo dàxué jiāo Zhōngwén
Wáng yī·shēng	zài zhèige yīyuàn gōngzuò
wǒ mèimei	zài zhèige zhōngxué xué·xí
Lǐ nǚshì	zài zhèr gōngzuò

女士 nǚshì Ms.   工作 gōngzuò To work (one's job)

I. Mini Dialogs: Full Characters and English

1. A. 麗麗，來見見我的朋友。

    B. 好啊！

    A. 這是麗麗、我女兒。

    C. 見到你很高興。

    A. 這是彼得，剛從美國來。

    A. Lili, come meet a friend of mine.
    B. O.K.
    A. This is my daughter, Lili.
    C. I'm pleased to meet you.
    A. This is Peter. He just arrived from America.

2. A. 這位是美國大學的校長、布朗博士。
    這位是兒童醫院院長、林女士。

    B. 你好！

    C. 你好！

    A. This is Dr. Brown, the president of American University.
    This is Ms. Lin, the head of the Children's Hospital.
    B. How do you do.
    C. How do you do.

高兴 gāo∘xìng
      To be happy.

校长 xiàozhǎng
      The head of a school.

J. MINI DIALOGS: SIMPLIFIED CHARACTERS AND PINYIN

1.

A. 丽丽，来见见我的朋友。

B. 好啊！

A. 这是丽丽，我女儿。

C. 见到你很高兴。

A. 这是彼得，刚从美国来。

A. Lìli, lái jiànjian wǒde péngyou.
B. Hǎo a.
A. Zhèi shì Lìli, wǒ nǚér.
C. Jiàn dào nǐ hěn gāoxing.
A. Zhèi shì Bǐdé, gāng cóng Meiguo lái.

2.

A. 这位是美国大学的校长、布朗博士。

这位是儿童医院院长、林女士。

B. 你好！

C. 你好！

A. Zhèiwei shì Měiguo dàxué de xiàozhǎng, Bùláng bóshi.
Zhèiwei shì értóng yīyuàn yuànzhǎng, Lín nǚshì.
B. Nǐ hǎo.
C. Nǐ hǎo.

博士   bó·shì
        Dr. (Ph.D.)   医院院长   yīyuàn yuànzhǎng
                                             The head of a hospital.

I (2)

3. A. 湯姆，你來，我給你介紹一位朋友。

   B. 好。

   A. 這是…

   B. 啊，這是王麗麗。我們認識的。
      不必介紹了。

   A. Come here, Tom. I want to introduce you to a friend.
     B. O.K.
   A. This is ...
     B. Oh, it's Wang Lili! We already know each other.
        You don't have to introduce us.

4. A. 這位是梁同志，
      外號是"活字典"。
      他甚麼都知道。
   B. 別開玩笑了。

   A. This is Comrade Liang.
      His nickname is 'Living Dictionary'.
      He knows everything.
     B. Stop kidding around.

认识	rèn‧shì To know someone.	同志	tóngzhì Comrade.
字典	zìdiǎn Dictionary.	别	bié Don't.

* Notice the principle for ordering the vocabulary: first line across both pages and then the second line, as shown by the numbers to the right.

p 14		p 15	
1	2	3	4
5	6	7	8

J (2)

3.
A. 汤姆，你来，我给你介绍一位朋友。

B. 好。

A. 这是···

B. 啊，这是王丽丽，我们认识的。
   不必介绍了。

A. Tāngmǔ, nǐ lái, wǒ gěi nǐ jièshào yíwèi péngyou.
B. Hǎo.
A. Zhèi shì ···
B. À, zhèi shì Wáng Lìli, wǒmen rènshi de.
   Búbì jièshào le.

4.
A. 这位是梁同志，
   外号是"活字典"。
   他什么都知道。

B. 别开玩笑了。

A. Zhèiwei shì Liáng tóngzhì.
   Wàihào shì 'Huó Zìdiǎn'.
   Tā shémme dōu zhīdào.
B. Bié kāi wánxiào le.

外号	wàihào Nickname.	活	huó Live.
玩笑	wánxiào A joke.	开玩笑	kāi wánxiào To make a joke.

K. CULTURAL NOTES

Chinese names. The surname (usually a single character, but occasionally two) precedes the given name (usually two characters, but sometimes one). Children take their father's surname. A married woman does not take her husband's surname.

Foreign names. The commonest foreign names have been given standard Chinese readings and can be found in the back of some dictionaries published in China. Tom Green, for example, is Tāngmǔ Gélín.[a] (Notice the use of the dot between the given name and surname in the character writing.)

Terms of address. The titles xiānsheng[b] (Mr.), tàitai[c] (Mrs.), nǚshì[d] (Ms.), and xiǎojiě[e] (Miss) are not commonly used in China today. They are frequently used when addressing and referring to foreigners, however, and in some formal situations they can be used with Chinese names. The commonest way to address a Chinese acquaintance is to use the full name (Lǐ Tài-píng[f]). If the person is much older than the speaker, lǎo[g] is often used before the surname (Lǎo Lǐ[h]), and if the person is much younger, xiǎo[i] can be used (Xiǎo Lǐ[j]). If the person has a particular title (like Dr.), it is used after the surname (Lǐ Yīsheng[k]). The given name alone is used only with family members and very close friends; and if it is a single character, it is sometimes avoided even then. (Note that we use the given name Àiméi[l] to identify the wife in the dialogs, but the surname Wáng[m] for the husband, who has a single-character first name.)

a. 汤姆·格林   e. 小姐   i. 小

b. 先生   f. 李太平   j. 小李

c. 太太   g. 老   k. 李医生

d. 女士   h. 老李   l. 爱梅

m. 王

LESSON 2

INTRODUCING ONESELF

自 我 介 绍

A. Dialog: Pinyin Transcription

Tāngmǔ: Wǒ lái zìwǒ jièshào yixià.[1] Wǒ jiào[2] Tom Green.   1

         Wǒde Zhōngguo péngyou jiào wǒ Tāngmǔ.   2

         Wǒ shì Měiguo Yánhúchéng rén.   3

         Qùnián déle jiāo Yīngwén de shuòshì xuéwèi.   4

         Xiànzài zài Zhōngguo de Běifāng dàxué jiāo Yīngwén.   5

Ānnā: Wǒ shì Anna Green. Wǒde Zhōngwén míngzi[2] shì Ānnā.   6

         Nǐmen jiào wǒ Ānnā déle.[3] Wǒde zhuānyè shì jiàoyu.   7

         Yǒule háizi yǐhòu, wǒ bu gōngzuòle.   8

         Wǒ děi zhàogu háizi.   9

Àiméi: Wǒ xìng[2] Mǎ, jiào[2] Mǎ Àiméi, értóng yīyuàn de yīsheng. 10

Wáng: Wǒ buyòng zìwǒ jièshào le ba?   11

         Nǐmen dōu zhīdào wǒ shì Wáng Píng, Běijīng rén,   12

         wǔshí suìle. Haha ···, bubì jièshàole ba?   13

Zhòng: Bubìle, bubìle.   14

Wáng: Duìle,[4]   15

         nǐmen liǎngwèi de Zhōngguo huà jiǎng de zhēn bucuò ya.   16

Tāngmǔ: À, mámahuhū. Wǒmen zài Měiguo xuéle sān nián.   17

Ānnā: Zài Zhōngguo wǒmen hái yào jìxu xué ne.   18

B. Dialog: Simplified Characters

汤姆: 我来自我介绍一下[1]，我叫[2] Tom Green.   1
我的中国朋友叫我汤姆。   2
我是美国盐湖城人。   3
去年得了教英文的硕士学位。   4
现在在中国的北方大学教英文。   5

安娜: 我是 Anna Green. 我的中文名字[2]是安娜，   6
你们叫我安娜得了[3]。我的专业是教育。   7
有了孩子以后，我不工作了。   8
我得照顾孩子。   9

爱梅: 我姓[2]马，叫[2]马爱梅，儿童医院的医生。   10

王: 我不用自我介绍了吧？   11
你们都知道我是王平，北京人，   12
五十岁了，哈哈…，不必介绍了吧？   13

众: 不必了，不必了。   14

王: 对了[4]，   15
你们两位的中国话讲得真不错呀！   16

汤姆: 啊，马马虎虎．我们在美国学了三年。   17

安娜: 在中国我们还要继续学呢。   18

C. Dialog: Yale Transcription

Tāngmǔ: Wǒ lái dzwǒ jyèshàu yisyà.[1] Wǒ jyàu[2] Tom Green.   1

Wǒde Jūnggwo péngyou jyàu wǒ Tāngmǔ.   2

Wǒ shr̀ Měigwo Yánhúchéng rén.   3

Chyù nyán déle jyāu Yīngwén de shwòshr̀ sywéwèi.   4

Syàndzài dzài Jūnggwo de Běifāng dàsywé jyāu Yīngwén.   5

Ānnā: Wǒ shr̀ Anna Green. Wǒde Jūngwén míngdz[2] shr̀ Ānnā.   6

Nǐmen jyàu wǒ Ānnā déle.[3] Wǒde jwānyè shr̀ jyàuyu.   7

Yǒule háidz yǐhòu, wǒ bu gūngdzwòle.   8

Wǒ děi jàugu háidz.   9

Àiméi: Wǒ syìng[2] Mǎ, jyàu[2] Mǎ Àiméi, értúng yīywàn de yīsheng. 10

Wáng: Wǒ buyùng dzwǒ jyèshàu le ba?   11

Nǐmen dōu jīdàu wǒ shr̀ Wáng Píng, Běijīng rén,   12

wǔshr̀ swèile. Haha ···, bubì jyèshàule ba?   13

Jùng: Bubìle, bubìle.   14

Wáng: Dwèile,[4]   15

nǐmen lyǎngwèi de Jūnggwo hwà jyǎng de jēn butswò ya. 16

Tāngmǔ: À, mámahuhū. Wǒmen dzài Měigwo sywéle sān nyán.   17

Ānnā: Dzài Jūnggwo wǒmen hái yàu jìsyu sywé ne.   18

D. DIALOG: FULL CHARACTERS

湯姆: 我來自我介紹一下[1]，我叫[2]Tom Green.   1
我的中國朋友叫我湯姆。   2
我是美國鹽湖城人。   3
去年得了教英文的碩士學位。   4
現在在中國的北方大學教英文。   5

安娜: 我是Anna Green.我的中文名字[2]是安娜。   6
你們叫我安娜得了[3]。我的專業是教育。   7
有了孩子以後，我不工作了。   8
我得照顧孩子。   9

愛梅: 我姓[2]馬，叫[2]馬愛梅，兒童醫院的醫生。   10

王: 我不用自我介紹了吧？   11
你們都知道我是王平，北京人，   12
五十歲了，哈哈…，不必介紹了吧？   13

眾: 不必了，不必了。   14

王: 對了[4]，   15
你們兩位的中國話講得真不錯呀！   16

湯姆: 啊，馬馬虎虎，我們在美國學了三年。   17

安娜: 在中國我們還要繼續學呢。   18

E. Dialog: Vocabulary and Notes

自我   zìwǒ
Myself.

硕士   shuòshì
Master's degree.

学位   xuéwèi
Academic degree.

专业   zhuānyè
Specialty, major.

教育   jiào‧yù
Education.

照顾   zhào‧gù
To look after.

不用   búyòng
Not necessary.

不错   búcuò
Not bad,
pretty good.

马马虎虎   mámahuhū
So so.

继续   jì‧xù
To continue.

呢   ne
Shows
continuation.

1. lái jièshào yixià.[a] This is like jièshào jièshào[b] and
jièshào yi jièshào.[c] These three structures add very little
to the meaning of the verb. They simply make the sentence
less abrupt. It is something like 'give it a try' or 'have a
go at it' in English.

2. xìng;[d] míng,[e] míng‧zi;[f] jiào.[g] The first of these refers
specifically to the surname, and the second and third refer
to the given name. The best way to refer to the *full* name is
with the fourth (to call or name). Nǐ jiào shémme míngzi?[h]
Wǒ jiào Mǎ Àiméi.[i]

3. déle.[j] This indicates a suggestion: 'Why don't you ...'.

4. Duì le.[k] This signals a change of subject: 'By the way,'.

a. 来介绍一下   d. 姓   g. 叫   j. 得了
b. 介绍介绍   e. 名   h. 你叫什么名字   k. 对了
c. 介绍一介绍   f. 名字   i. 我叫马爱梅

F. DIALOG: ENGLISH

Tom: Let me introduce myself. My name's Tom Green.   1

        My Chinese friends call me Tāngmǔ.   2

        I'm an American from Salt Lake City.   3

        Last year I got an M.A. in teaching English.   4

        Now I'm teaching English at China's Northern University. 5

Anna: I'm Anna Green. My Chinese name is Ānnā.   6

        You can call me Ānnā. My field is education.   7

        But I haven't worked since I had my baby.   8

        I've had to take care of him.   9

Aimei: My name is Ma, Ma Aimei, a doctor at the Children's Hospital. 10

Wang: I don't have to introduce myself, do I?   11

        You all know I'm Wang Ping, from Peking,   12

        fifty years old. Haha ···, is this necessary?   13

All: No. We all know you.   14

Wang: By the way,   15

        you both speak Chinese very well.   16

Tom: Oh, we just get by. We studied three years in America. 17

Anna: We're going to continue studying it in China, too.   18

G. SUBSTITUTIONS: FULL CHARACTERS AND ENGLISH

1.

你是<u>哪裏</u>人？
我是<u>美國</u>人。
　日本
　德國
　英國
　澳大利亞
　法國
　加拿大
　蘇聯
　鹽湖城
　紐約
　倫敦
　洛杉磯

巴黎
莫斯科
芝加哥
悉尼
東京
香港
舊金山
新加坡
北京
上海
南京
廣東
廣州

Where are you from?
I'm from <u>America</u> .
　　　Japan
　　　Germany
　　　England
　　　Australia
　　　France
　　　Canada
　　　Russia
　　　Salt Lake City
　　　New York
　　　London
　　　Los Angeles

Paris
Moscow
Chicago
Sidney
Tokyo
Hong Kong
San Francisco
Singapore
Peking
Shanghai
Nanking
Guangdong
Canton

H. Substitutions: Simplified Characters and Pinyin

1.

你是<u>哪里</u>人？   巴黎
我是<u>美国</u>人。   莫斯科
　　　日本   芝加哥
　　　德国   悉尼
　　　英国   东京
　　　澳大利亚   香港
　　　法国   旧金山
　　　加拿大   新加坡
　　　苏联   北京
　　　盐湖城   上海
　　　纽约   南京
　　　伦敦   广东
　　　洛杉矶   广州

Nǐ shì <u>nǎlǐ</u> rén?   Bālí
Wǒ shì <u>Měiguo</u> rén.   Mòsīkē
　　　Rìběn   Zhījiāgē
　　　Déguo   Xīní
　　　Yīngguo   Dōngjīng
　　　Àodàlìyǎ   Xiānggǎng
　　　Fàguo   Jiùjīnshān
　　　Jiānádà   Xīnjiāpō
　　　Sūlián   Běijīng
　　　Yánhúchéng   Shànghai
　　　Niǔyuē   Nánjīng
　　　Lúndūn   Guǎngdōng
　　　Luòshānjī   Guǎngzhōu

G (2)

2. 我的專業是教育。   語言學
         生物   人類學
         化學   國際貿易
         商業   文科
         歷史   理科
         物理   工科
         經濟   醫科

My field is education.   linguistics
         biology   anthropology
         chemistry   international trade
         business   humanities
         history   science
         physics   engineering
         economics   medicine

3. 我去年得了教英語的碩士學位。
         化學   博士
   我是去年新聞系的畢業生。
   我是美國大學電機系的畢業生。

Last year I got an M.A. in teaching English.
             a Ph.D.   chemistry
Last year I graduated from the journalism department.
I'm a graduate from the electrical engineering department
                                    of American University.

H (2)

2.

我的专业是<u>教育</u>。　　　　语言学
　　　　　生物　　　　　　　人类学
　　　　　化学　　　　　　　国际贸易
　　　　　商业　　　　　　　文科
　　　　　历史　　　　　　　理科
　　　　　物理　　　　　　　工科
　　　　　经济　　　　　　　医科

Wǒde zhuānyè shì <u>jiào‧yù</u>.　　　yǔyánxué
　　　　　　　　shēngwù　　　　rénlèixué
　　　　　　　　huàxué　　　　　guójì mào‧yì
　　　　　　　　shāngyè　　　　wénkē
　　　　　　　　lìshǐ　　　　　lǐkē
　　　　　　　　wùlǐ　　　　　gōngkē
　　　　　　　　jīngjì　　　　　yīkē

3.

我去年得了<u>教英语</u>的<u>硕士</u>学位。
　　　　　化学　　　博士
我是去年<u>新闻</u>系的<u>毕业生</u>。
我是美国大学<u>电机</u>系的<u>毕业生</u>

Wǒ qù nián déle <u>jiāo Yīngwén</u> de <u>shuòshì</u> xuéwèi.
　　　　　　　　　huàxué　　　　bóshì
Wǒ shì qù nián <u>xīn wén</u> xì de <u>bìyè shēng</u>.
Wǒ shì Měiguo dàxué <u>diànjī</u> xì de <u>bìyè shēng</u>.

I. Mini Dialogs: Full Characters and English

1.
A. 我是林大文，你是…?

B. 我是愛琳·布朗。

A. I'm Lin Dawen. You're ... ?
B. I'm Eileen Brown.

2.
A. 小朋友，你叫甚麼名字?

B. 我叫艾麗絲，你呢?

A. 我叫王麗麗。

A. What's your name, little friend?
B. My name's Alice. And yours?
A. My name's Lili Wang.

3.
A. 高先生，你好?

B. 對不起，我不姓高，我姓李。

A. 啊呀，認錯人了。

A. How are you, Mr. Gao?
B. I beg your pardon. My name's not Gao. It's Li.
A. Oh, sorry. My mistake.

错   cuò
Mistaken, wrong.

认错   rèn cuò
To recognize wrongly.

J. MINI DIALOGS: SIMPLIFIED CHARACTERS AND PINYIN

1.
A. 我是林大文，你是…？

B. 我是爱琳·布朗。

A. Wǒ shì Lín Dàwén. Nǐ shì ... ?
B. Wǒ shì Àilín Bùláng.

2.
A. 小朋友，你叫什么名字？

B. 我叫艾丽丝，你呢？

A. 我叫王丽丽。

A. Xiǎo péngyou, nǐ jiào shémme míngzi?
B. Wǒ jiào Àilìsī. Nǐ ne?
A. Wǒ jiào Wáng Lìli.

3.
A. 高先生，你好？

B. 对不起，我不姓高，我姓李。

A. 啊呀，认错人了。

A. Gāo xiānsheng, nǐ hǎo?
B. Duìbuqǐ, wǒ bu xìng Gāo. Wǒ xìng Lǐ.
A. Āyà, rèn cuò rén le.

I (2)

4.
A. 我是李太平，
你是王教授吧？

B. 你認錯人了吧，我不是教授。

A. 對不起，對不起。

A. I'm Li Taiping.
You're Professor Wang, aren't you?
B. You've made a mistake. I'm not a professor.
A. Oh, sorry! I'm sorry!

5.
A. 您好，我是懷特醫生、外科大夫。
兒童醫院請我來講學一個月。
您貴姓？

B. 我姓林，
這個醫院的內科醫生。

A. Hello. I'm Dr. White. I'm a surgeon.
The Children's Hospital invited me to come lecture for a
month. May I ask your name?
B. My name's Lin.
I'm a doctor at this hospital.

外科	wàikē Surgical department.	大夫	dài‧fū A doctor.
內科	nèikē Department of internal medicine.		

J (2)

4.
> A. 我是李太平，
>   你是王教授吧？
>   B. 你认错人了吧，我不是教授。
> A. 对不起，对不起。
>
> A. Wǒ shì Lǐ Tàipíng.
>   Nǐ shì Wáng jiàoshòu ba?
>   B. Nǐ rèn cuò rén le ba. Wǒ bushì jiàoshòu.
> A. Duìbuqǐ, duìbuqǐ.

5.
> A. 您好，我是怀特医生、外科大夫。
>   儿童医院请我来讲学一个月。
>   您贵姓？
>   B. 我姓林。
>   这个医院的内科医生。
>
> A. Nín hǎo, wǒ shì Huáitè yīsheng, wàikē dàifu.
>   Értóng yīyuàn qǐng wǒ lái jiǎngxué yīge yuè.
>   Nín guì xìng?
>   B. Wǒ xìng Lín.
>   Zhèige yīyuàn de nèikē yīsheng.

讲学   jiǎngxué
      To lecture.

贵姓   guì xìng
      Your honorable surname.

K. CULTURAL NOTES

Embarrassing questions. In most cultures a period of asking
questions often follows the introductions, as the people try to
learn more about each other. But the nature of these questions
may vary from culture to culture. A question that shows friendly
interest in one culture might be quite impolite or irritating in
another. For the Chinese, 'How old are you?' and 'Are you married yet?' (followed by 'Why not?' if you aren't and 'How many
children have you got?' if you are) simply show friendly interest.
For many Westerners, however, these questions are considered impolite. If you prefer not to answer questions like these, you
should be prepared with friendly dodges. Sharp or sarcastic
comebacks that you use with 'rude' Westerners would be quite out
of place.

Need for a self introduction. Chinese probably have more of
a need than Westerners to know about the lives of the people they
associate with. Their interpersonal feelings tend to run deeper.
This explains the questions of the preceding paragraph. But that
paragraph was talking about the average Chinese—farmers and the
man in the street. The Chinese intellectual feels the same need
to get this kind of information from the people he talks to; but
he knows that Westerners might resent his questions, so he tends
to overcompensate and avoid all personal questions. Here is
where the Westerner's self introduction comes in. He must volun-
teer personal information about himself.

Laughing and giggling. Laughing may be used for different
purposes in different cultures. As a foreigner in China, you
will constantly encounter a laughter that shows friendly interest
in foreigners. You should not mistake this for mocking or ridi-
cule. And you will sometimes get a laugh or giggle in response
to your questions (especially when the person is with his or her
friends). This laugh probably shows that the person hasn't understood your English or bad Chinese. A response (or at least
some reaction) is obviously called for, but the person can't pos-
sibly respond (since he hasn't understood you). The laugh or
giggle is simply a pleasant substitute reaction. Professor Wang
Ping's laugh in the dialog is another example of the same sort of
thing.

LESSON 3

USING THE TELEPHONE

打 电 话

A. Dialog: Pinyin Transcription

Tāngmǔ:	(Bō 890951[1], jiētōng hòu, duì jiēxiànyuán shuō:)	1
	Qǐng jiē 345 fēnjī.	2
X:	Wéi.	3
Tāngmǔ:	Wèi. Wáng jiàoshòu zài ma?	4
X:	Qǐng děngyideng.	5
Wáng:	Wéi. Wǒ shì Wáng Píng. Nǐ shì shéi ya?	6
Tāngmǔ:	Hài! Wáng jiàoshòu. Wǒ shì Tāngmǔ.	7
Wáng:	À! Nǐ hǎo.	8
Tāngmǔ:	Jīntiān xiàwǔ nǐ yǒu kòng ma?	9
	Wǒ xiǎng hé nǐ jiànjian miàn.	10
Wáng:	Hǎo a! Hss[2]···ēn, āyà, jīntiān xiàwǔ wǒ yǒu shì.	11
	Míngtiān shàngwǔ xíng ma?	12
Tāngmǔ:	Xíng. Míngtiān shàngwǔ jiǔ diǎnzhōng,	13
	wǒ dào nǐ bàngōngshì qù, hǎo ma?	14
Wáng:	Hǎo. Wǒ zài nàr děng nǐ.	15
Tāngmǔ:	Hǎo. Míngtiān jiàn.	16

B. DIALOG: SIMPLIFIED CHARACTERS

汤姆: （拨 890951[1]. 接通后，对接线员说:)   1
请接 345 分机。   2

X: 喂！   3

汤姆: 喂！王教授在吗？   4

X: 请等一等。   5

王: 喂，我是王平。你是谁呀？   6

汤姆: 嗨，王教授，我是汤姆。   7

王: 啊！你好。   8

汤姆: 今天下午你有空吗？   9
我想和你见见面。   10

王: 好啊！唑…[2]嗯，啊呀。今天下午我有事.   11
明天上午行吗？   12

汤姆: 行。明天上午九点钟，   13
我到你办公室去，好吗？   14

王: 好，我在那儿等你。   15

汤姆: 好，明天见。   16

C. Dialog: Yale Transcription

Tāngmǔ: (Bwō 890951[1], jyētūng hòu, dwèi jyēsyànywán shwō:)   1

Chǐng jyē 345 fēnjī.   2

X: Wéi.   3

Tāngmǔ: Wèi. Wáng jyàushòu dzài ma?   4

X: Chǐng děngyideng.   5

Wáng: Wéi. Wǒ shr̀ Wáng Píng. Nǐ shr̀ shéi ya?   6

Tāngmǔ: Hài! Wáng jyàushòu. Wǒ shr̀ Tāngmǔ.   7

Wáng: À! Nǐ hǎu.   8

Tāngmǔ: Jīntyān syàwǔ nǐ yǒu kùng ma?   9

Wǒ syǎng hé nǐ jyànjyan myàn.   10

Wáng: Hǎu a! Hss[2]...ēn, āyà, jīntyān syàwǔ wǒ yǒu shr̀.   11

Míngtyān shàngwǔ syíng ma?   12

Tāngmǔ: Syíng. Míngtyān shàngwǔ jyǒu dyǎnjūng,   13

wǒ dàu nǐ bàngūngshr̀ chyù, hǎu ma?   14

Wáng: Hǎu. Wǒ dzài nàr děng nǐ.   15

Tāngmǔ: Hǎu. Míngtyān jyàn.   16

D. DIALOG: FULL CHARACTERS

湯姆: （撥 890951[1].   接通後，對接綫員說:）   1

請 接 345 分機。   2

X: 喂！   3

湯姆: 喂！王教授在嗎？   4

X: 請 等 一 等。   5

王: 喂！我是王平，你是誰呀？   6

湯姆: 嗨！王教授，我是湯姆。   7

王: 啊！你好。   8

湯姆: 今天下午你有空嗎？   9

我 想 和 你 見 見 面。   10

王: 好啊，嗯[2]…嗯，啊呀。今天下午我有事。   11

明天上午行嗎？   12

湯姆: 行，明天上午九點鐘，   13

我到你辦公室去，好嗎？   14

王: 好，我在那兒等你。   15

湯姆: 好，明天見。   16

E. DIALOG: VOCABULARY AND NOTES

电话   diànhuà
A telephone.

打电话   dǎ diànhuà
To telephone.

拨   bō
To dial.

接   jiē
To connect.

接通   jiētōng
To make a
connection.

接线员   jiēxiànyuán
A telephone
operator.

分机   fēnjī
A telephone
extension.

喂   wèi, wéi
Hello
(on the phone).

等   děng
To wait.

下午   xiàwǔ
Afternoon.

有空   yǒu kòng
To have free time,
be free.

见面   jiànmiàn
To meet
or see someone.

有事   yǒu shì
To have business,
be busy.

上午   shàngwǔ
Morning.

行   xíng
Can do, can be done.

点钟   diǎnzhōng
O'clock.

办公室   bàngōngshì
An office.

1. When speaking on the phone, <u>yāo</u>[a] is usually used instead of <u>yī</u>[b] for clarity (<u>yī</u>[b] might be confused with <u>qī</u>[c]).

2. <u>hss</u>.[d] This stands for the sound of air being sucked in through the teeth. At first Wang is happy at the chance of seeing Tom (<u>Hǎo a!</u>[e]). Then he thinks of something that might interfere (<u>hss</u>) and hesitates a second (<u>ēn</u>[f]). Then he shows his disappointment (<u>āyà</u>[g]) as he explains.

   a. 幺   c. 七   e. 好啊   g. 啊呀

   b. 一   d. 咝   f. 嗯

F. Dialog: English

Tom:	(To the operator, after dialing and getting 890951:)	1
	Please give me extension 345.	2
X:	Hello.	3
Tom:	Hello. Is Professor Wang there?	4
X:	Please wait a minute.	5
Wang:	Hello. This is Wang Ping. Who's speaking, please?	6
Tom:	Ah! Professor Wang. This is Tom.	7
Wang:	Oh, hi.	8
Tom:	Are you going to be free this afternoon?	9
	I'd like to see you.	10
Wang:	Fine! Oh, gee, I've got something to do this afternoon.	11
	Can you make it tomorrow morning?	12
Tom:	Sure. Tomorrow morning at 9 o'clock	13
	I'll come to your office. O.K.?	14
Wang:	Fine. I'll wait for you there.	15
Tom:	Good. See you tomorrow.	16

G. Substitutions: Full Characters and English

1. 喂，王平？   你是王平嗎？
   王平嗎？   你是不是王平？

   Hello. <u>Wang Ping?</u>   Is that Wang Ping?
           Wang Ping?   Is that Wang Ping?

2. A. 王平嗎？ B. 是啊。
                    我就是。
                    我就是王平。
                    不是，我是小王。

   A. Wang Ping?   B. <u>Yes.</u>
                       This is he.
                       This is Wang Ping.
                       No, this is Little Wang.

3. A. 麗麗在嗎？ B. 我就是。
                     請等一等。
                     她剛走。
                     不在，一會兒就來。

   A. Is Lili there?   B. <u>This is she.</u>
                          Please wait a minute.
                          She just left.
                          No, but she'll be back soon.

H. SUBSTITUTIONS: SIMPLIFIED CHARACTERS AND PINYIN

1.
喂，<u>王平</u>？   你是王平吗？
王平吗？   你是不是王平？

Wèi. <u>Wáng Píng?</u>   Nǐ shì Wáng Píng ma?
Wáng Píng ma?   Nǐ shì bu shi Wáng Píng?

2.
A. 王平吗？   B. <u>是啊</u>.
我就是。
我就是王平。
不是，我是小王。

A. Wáng Píng ma? B. <u>Shì a.</u>
Wǒ jiùshi.
Wǒ jiùshi Wáng Píng.
Búshi, wǒ shì Xiǎo Wáng.

3.
A. 丽丽在吗？   B. <u>我就是</u>。
请等一等。
她刚走。
不在，一会儿就来。

A. Lìli zài ma?   B. <u>Wǒ jiùshi.</u>
Qǐng děng yideng.
Tā gāng zǒu.
Bú zài, yi huěr jiù lái.

I. MINI DIALOGS: FULL CHARACTERS AND ENGLISH

1.
A. 喂！

B. 喂！你是不是小王？

A. 是啊。

B. 你父親在家嗎？

A. 他不在家。要他給你回個電話嗎？

B. 唔…我再給他打吧。

A. Hello.
  B. Hello. Is that Little Wang?
A. Yes.
  B. Is your father there?
A. No he isn't. Do you want him to call you back?
  B. Oh, I'll call again later.

2.
A. 麗麗！

B. 哎。

A. 你的電話。

B. 好。謝謝。

A. Lili!
  B. Yes.
A. Telephone.
  B. O.K. Thanks.

回 电 话   huí diànhuà
To return a phone call.

J. Mini Dialogs: Simplified Characters and Pinyin

1.
> A. 喂！
>
> 　B. 喂！你是不是小王？
>
> A. 是啊。
>
> 　B. 你父亲在家吗？
>
> A. 他不在家。要他给你回个电话吗？
>
> 　B. 嗯…我再给他打吧。

A. Wéi.
　B. Wèi.　Nǐ shìbushi xiǎo Wáng?
A. Shì a.
　B. Nǐ fùqin zài jiā ma?
A. Tā bu zài jiā.　Yào tā gěi nǐ huí ge diànhuà ma?
　B. Mmm···　wǒ zài gěi tā dǎ ba.

2.
> A. 丽丽！
>
> 　B. 哎。
>
> A. 你的电话。
>
> 　B. 好。谢谢。

A. Lìli!
　B. Ài.
A. Nǐde diànhuà.
　B. Hǎo.　Xièxie.

再　　zài
　　　Again.

打 is short for 打电话

I (2)

3.
A. 喂！
   B. 愛梅嗎？
A. 是啊。
   B. 今天晚上我晚一點兒回家。
A. 嗯。

A. Hello.
  B. Aimei?
A. Yes.
  B. I'll be home a little late this evening.
A. O.K.

4.
A. 喂。
   B. 喂，你是誰？
A. 你找誰？
   B. 找王平。
A. 我就是。喂？喂？喂？
   哼！電話斷了。

A. Hello.
  B. Hello. Who's this?
A. Who are you calling?
  B. I want to talk to Wang Ping.
A. This is he. Hello? Hello? Hello?
   Darn it! We've been cut off.

晚   wǎn   晚上   wǎnshàng
      To be late.   Evening.

J (2)

3.
A. 喂！

　B. 爱梅吗？

A. 是啊。

　B. 今天晚上我晚一点儿回家。

A. 嗯。

A. Wéi.
　B. Àiméi ma?
A. Shì a.
　B. Jīntiān wǎnshàng wǒ wǎn yidiǎr huí jiā.
A. Ēn.

4.
A. 喂！

　B. 喂. 你是谁？

A. 你找谁？

　B. 找王平。

A. 我就是。喂？喂？喂？

　哼！电话断了。

A. Wéi.
　B. Wèi. Nǐ shì shéi?
A. Nǐ zhǎo shéi?
　B. Zhǎo Wáng Píng.
A. Wǒ jiùshì. Wéi? Wéi? Wéi?
　Hèng! Diànhuà duànle.

断　duàn
　　To break or cut off.

I (3)

5.
A. 喂 !

B. 喂，馬愛梅在嗎 ?

A. 不在。

B. 去哪兒了 ?

A. 不知道。你要留話嗎 ?

B. 我是她愛人、王平。

讓她給我回個電話，好嗎 ?

A. 好。

A. Hello.
  B. Hello. Is Ma Aimei there?
A. No she isn't.
  B. Where has she gone?
A. I don't know. Do you want to leave a message?
  B. This is her husband, Wang Ping.
    Can you tell her to call me back?
A. Sure.

6.
A. 喂.

B. 喂，我找麗麗。

A. 你打錯了。這兒沒有麗麗。

A. Hello.
  B. Hello. I want to talk to Lili.
A. You've got the wrong number. There's no Lili here.

留話 liú huà
To leave a message.

让 ràng
To have someone do something.

J (3)

5.
A. 喂！

   B. 喂，马爱梅在吗？

A. 不在。

   B. 去哪儿了？

A. 不知道。你要留话吗？

   B. 我是她爱人、王平。

     让她给我回个电话，好吗？

A. 好。

A. Wéi.
  B. Wèi. Mǎ Àiméi zài ma?
A. Bú zài.
  B. Qù nǎrle?
A. Bù zhīdào. Nǐ yào liúhuà ma?
  B. Wǒ shì tā àirén, Wáng Píng.
    Ràng tā gěi wǒ huí ge diànhuà, hǎo ma?
A. Hǎo.

6.
A. 喂。

   B. 喂，我找丽丽。

A. 你打错了。这儿没有丽丽。

A. Wéi.
  B. Wèi. Wǒ zhǎo Lìli.
A. Nǐ dǎ cuòle. Zhèr méiyǒu Lìli.

打错   dǎ cuò
     To dial or call a wrong number

K. Cultural Notes

Many Americans will initiate a few sentences of small talk between the hellos and the message of telephone calls. The Chinese are much less likely to do this. But the American will probably not think that the Chinese is being impolite when he goes straight to the purpose of the call. If he thinks about it at all, he will probably think that Chinese have different customs. But *un*conscious behavior is another matter. When the caller identifies himself ('This is Tom', for example), the American may say anything from 'Oh, Tom' to a long sentence telling how delighted he is to hear from him. But whatever the American says, he will almost surely say it with a *raised voice*. The Chinese will not normally raise his voice in this situation (at least not nearly as much as Americans do), and the American is far more likely to feel offended at a lack of enthusiasm on the part of the Chinese than to realize that the Chinese have different customs.

Two more differences between Chinese and American phone calls lie somewhere between the very conscious small talk and the unconscious raising of the voice. The American will bring the phone call to an end gradually, with sentences like 'I've got to go now', or 'It's been nice talking to you', or 'Thanks for calling'. And he will almost surely finish with something that clearly shows he is going to hang up: 'Goodbye', 'Thanks', or 'O.K.'—depending on the circumstances. The Chinese may finish with zài jiàn,[a] but very often the signal is nothing more than something like en en[b] or hao hao hao,[b] and the American might think he was cut off. The main point to remember is that customs differ. And in this case, 'abrupt' does not mean 'impolite'.

a. 再见   b. 嗯嗯   c. 好好好

LESSON 4

APOLOGIES AND REGRETS

道 歉 和 遺 憾

A. Dialog: Pinyin Transcription.

Tāngmǔ: Āiyà, Wáng jiàoshòu,   1

          qǐng yuánliang, wǒ lái chíle.   2

Wáng: Méi guānxi.   3

Tāngmǔ: Bànlùshàng chūzū qìchē huàile.   4

Wáng: Shì ma?   5

          Nǎ[1] nǐ zuò shémme chē láide ya?   6

Tāngmǔ: Wǒ gǎi zuò gōnggòng qìchē láide. Jǐ de yào sǐ.   7

Wáng: Zhēn zāogāo.   8

Tāngmǔ: Wèi shémme gōnggòng qìchē nàme jǐ ya?   9

Wáng: Zhēn bu qiǎo,   10

          zhèi shì jiāotōng gāo fēng shíjiān.   11

Tāngmǔ: Shì ma? Wǒ méi dānwu nǐde shíjiān ba?   12

Wáng: Ò! Tāngmǔ, méi shémme,   13

          wǒ zhīdào jiāotōng qíngkuàng.   14

          Béng shuōle.   15

          Qǐng zuò ba, xiē yi huěr.   16

B. DIALOG: SIMPLIFIED CHARACTERS

汤姆：　哎呀，王教授，　　　　　　　　　　1
　　　　请原谅，我来迟了。　　　　　　　　2

王：　　没关系。　　　　　　　　　　　　　3

汤姆：　半路上出租汽车坏了。　　　　　　　4

王：　　是吗？　　　　　　　　　　　　　　5
　　　　那你坐什么车来的呀？　　　　　　　6

汤姆：　我改坐公共汽车来的，挤得要死。　　7

王：　　真糟糕。　　　　　　　　　　　　　8

汤姆：　为什么公共汽车那么挤呀？　　　　　9

王：　　真不巧，　　　　　　　　　　　　　10
　　　　这是交通高峰时间。　　　　　　　　11

汤姆：　是吗？我没耽误你的时间吧？　　　　12

王：　　喔！汤姆，没什么，　　　　　　　　13
　　　　我知道交通情况，　　　　　　　　　14
　　　　甭说了，　　　　　　　　　　　　　15
　　　　请坐吧，歇一会儿。　　　　　　　　16

C. DIALOG: YALE TRANSCRIPTION

Tāngmǔ:	Āiyà, Wáng jyàushòu,	1
	chǐng ywánlyang, wǒ lái chǐle.	2
Wáng:	Méi gwānsyi.	3
Tāngmǔ:	Bànlùshàng chūdzū chǐchē hwàile.	4
Wáng:	Shr̀ ma?	5
	Nā[1] nǐ dzwò shémme chē láide ya?	6
Tāngmǔ:	Wǒ gǎi dzwò gūnggùng chǐchē láide. Jǐ de yàu sž.	7
Wáng:	Jēn dzāugāu.	8
Tāngmǔ:	Wèi shémme gūnggùng chǐchē nàme jǐ ya?	9
Wáng:	Jēn bu chyǎu,	10
	jèi shr̀ jyāutūng gāu fēng shŕjyān.	11
Tāngmǔ:	Shr̀ ma? Wǒ méi dānwu nǐde shŕjyān ba?	12
Wáng:	Ò! Tāngmǔ, méi shémme,	13
	wǒ jŕdàu jyāutūng chǐngkwàng.	14
	Béng shwōle.	15
	Chǐng dzwò ba, syē yi hwěr.	16

D. Dialog: Full Characters

湯姆: 哎呀，王教授，　　　　　　　　1
　　　請原諒，我來遲了。　　　　　　2

王:　　没關係。　　　　　　　　　　3

湯姆: 半路上出租汽車壞了。　　　　　4

王:　　是嗎？　　　　　　　　　　　5
　　　那[1]你坐甚麼車來的呀？　　　6

湯姆: 我改坐公共汽車來的，擠得要死。　7

王:　　真糟糕。　　　　　　　　　　8

湯姆: 為甚麼公共汽車那麼擠呀？　　　9

王:　　真不巧，　　　　　　　　　　10
　　　這是交通高峰時間。　　　　　　11

湯姆: 是嗎？我没耽誤你的時間吧？　　12

王:　　喔！湯姆，没甚麼，　　　　　13
　　　我知道交通情況，　　　　　　　14
　　　甭説了，　　　　　　　　　　　15
　　　請坐吧，歇一會兒。　　　　　　16

E. Dialog: Vocabulary and Notes

道歉　dào qiàn
To apologize.

遗憾　yíhàn
Regrets.

原谅　yuán·liàng
Excuse, forgive.

迟　chí
Late.

关系　guān·xì
Relationship.

没关系　méi guānxi
It doesn't matter.

半路　bànlù
On the way, midway.

出租汽车　chūzū qìchē
Taxi.

坐车　zuò chē
To ride (in a car, bus, etc.).

改　gǎi
To change.

公共汽车　gōnggòng qìchē
A public bus.

坏　huài
Spoil, break down.

挤　jǐ
Crowded.

死　sǐ
To die.

…得要死　… de yào sǐ
… to death.

糟糕　zāogāo
Too bad, what a mess.

巧　qiǎo
By lucky coincidence, opportune.

交通　jiāotōng
Communication, traffic.

峰　fēng
Peak.

耽误　dān·wù
Upset a schedule and waste time.

情况　qíngkuàng
Conditions, circumstances.

甭　béng
Short for 不用 (búyòng): not have to.

歇　xiē
To rest.

1. nǎ[a] = nàme[b]: then, in that case.

a. 那　　　b. 那么

F. Dialog: English

Tom: Oh, Professor Wang,   1

        please forgive me for coming so late.   2

Wang: It doesn't matter.   3

Tom: The taxi broke down on the way here.   4

Wang: Really?   5

        How did you get here, then?   6

Tom: I changed to a bus. It was so crowded I nearly died.   7

Wang: How awful!   8

Tom: Why would the bus have been so crowded?   9

Wang: You came at a bad time, unfortunately.   10

        This is the peak of the rush hour.   11

Tom: Really? I hope I haven't fouled up your schedule.   12

Wang: Oh, Tom, think nothing of it.   13

        I know what traffic conditions are like.   14

        Forget it!   15

        Sit down and rest a while.   16

G. Substitutions: Full Characters and English

1. 擠得要死。　　　　　　　　　　　熱
   餓　　　　　　　　　　　　　　　髒
   冷　　　　　　　　　　　　　　　鬧

   <u>It</u> was really <u>crowded</u> (to death).　　hot
   I　　　　　　 hungry　　　　　　　　dirty
   it　　　　　　 cold　　　　　　　　　 noisy

2. 為什麼公共汽車那麼擠呀 ?
   　　　出租汽車　　慢
   　　　火車　　　　鬧
   　　　船　　　　　髒

   Why was the <u>bus</u> so <u>crowded</u>?
   　　　　　 taxi　　slow
   　　　　　 train　 noisy
   　　　　　 boat　　dirty

3. 請原諒　我　　來遲了．
   對不起　　　打錯電話

   Please <u>forgive</u> me for <u>coming late</u>.
   　　　 excuse　　　　 dialing the wrong number

H. SUBSTITUTIONS: SIMPLIFIED CHARACTERS AND PINYIN

1. 挤得要死。　　　　　热
    饿　　　　　　　　脏
    冷　　　　　　　　闹

    Jǐ de yào sǐ.　　　　rè
    è　　　　　　　　zāng
    lěng　　　　　　　nào

2. 为什么 公共 汽车 那么 挤 呀?
    　　　出租汽车　慢
    　　　火车　　　闹
    　　　船　　　　脏

    Wèi shémme gōnggòng qìchē nàme jǐ ya?
    　　　　　　chūzū qìchē　　　　màn
    　　　　　　huǒchē　　　　　　nào
    　　　　　　chuán　　　　　　zāng

3. 请原谅　我　来迟了.
    对不起　　　打错电话

    Qǐng yuánliang wǒ lái chí le.
    duìbuqǐ　　　　dǎ cuò diànhuà

G (2)

4. 半路上<u>出租汽車</u>壞了。　　　　　　　　　　火車
        自行車　　　　　　　　　　　　　　船
        公共汽車　　　　　　　　　　　　汽車

    The <u>taxi</u> broke down on the way.   train
        bicycle   boat
        bus   car

5. <u>真糟糕</u>。　　　　　　　　　　　　　　不幸
        不巧　　　　　　　　　　　　　　可憐
        可惜　　　　　　　　　　　　　　可笑

    It's really <u>a mess</u>.   unfortunate
                inopportune   pitiful
                a pity   laughable

6. 我沒<u>耽誤你的</u>時間吧？
        浪費你的
        超過
        到

    Are you sure I didn't <u>interfere with your</u> time?
                          waste your
                          exceed the
                          use up the

H (2)

4.

半路上 <u>出租汽车</u> 坏了。   火车

    自行车   船

    公共汽车   汽车

Bànlùshang <u>chūzū qìchē</u> huài le.   huǒchē
    zìxíng chē   chuán
    gōnggòng qìchē   qìchē

5.

<u>真糟糕</u>,   不幸

    不巧   可怜

    可惜   可笑

Zhēn <u>zāogāo</u>.   buxìng
    bùqiǎo   kělián
    kěxī   kěxiào

6.

我没 <u>耽误</u> 你的时间吧？

    浪费你的

    超过

    到

Wǒ méi <u>dān•wù nǐde</u> shíjiān ba?
    làngfèi nǐde
    chāoguò
    dào

I. MINI DIALOGS: FULL CHARACTERS AND ENGLISH

1.
A. 你會説中國話嗎？

B. 過去會説一點兒，
現在差不多都忘了。

A. 多可惜呀！

A. Can you speak Chinese?
  B. I used to be able to speak a little,
     but now I've forgotten most of it.
A. What a pity!

2.
A. 那女孩兒的父母
在這次飛機失事中全死了。

B. 哎喲！真不幸。

A. That little girl's parents
   were both killed in this airplane crash.
  B. My gosh! How terrible.

过去	guòqù Past.	可惜	kěxī Regrettable.
飞机	fēijī Airplane.	失事	shīshì Accident.

J. MINI DIALOGS: SIMPLIFIED CHARACTERS AND PINYIN

1.
A. 你会说中国话吗？

B. 过去会说一点儿，
现在差不多都忘了。

A. 多可惜呀！

A. Nǐ huì shuō Zhōngguo huà ma?
B. Guòqù huì shuō yi diǎr,

2.
A. 那女孩儿的父母
在这次飞机失事中全死了。

B. 哎哟！真不幸。

A. Nà nǚhár de fùmǔ
zài zhèicì fēijī shīshì zhōng quán sǐle.
B. Āiyò! Zhēn búxìng.

全 quán
All.

中 zhōng
In, amidst; middle.

这次 zhèicì
This time.

不幸 búxìng
Unfortunately.

I (2)

3.
A. 對不起，我來遲了。
B. 沒甚麼，我也剛到。

A. Excuse me for coming late.
B. Never mind, I just got here myself.

4.
A. 昨天的音樂會好極了。
B. 真可惜，我沒去。

A. Yesterday's concert was really excellent.
B. What a pity I missed it.

5.
A. 對不起，我得早走一步了。
B. 吃了飯再走吧。
A. 不了，我惦着家裏的孩子呢。
B. 那我就不留你了。

A. I'm sorry. I have to leave early.
B. Can't you eat first?
A. No. I'm concerned about the kids at home.
B. Oh, I won't detain you, then.

音乐   yīnyuè   音乐会   yīnyuè huì
          Music.   Concert.

早走一步   zǎo zǒu yi bù   'To leave one step early.'
          To leave before someone else, or before expected.

J (2)

3.
A. 对不起，我来迟了 。
B. 没什么，我也刚到 。

A. Duìbuqǐ, wǒ lái chíle.
B. Méi shémme, wǒ yě gāng dào.

4.
A. 昨天的音乐会好极了 。
B. 真可惜，我没去 。

A. Zuótiān de yīnyuè huì hǎojíle.
B. Zhēn kěxī, wǒ méi qù.

5.
A. 对不起，我得早走一步了 。
B. 吃了饭再走吧 。
A. 不了，我惦着家里的孩子呢 。
B. 那我就不留你了 。

A. Duìbuqǐ, wǒ děi zǎo zǒu yíbù le.
B. Chīle fàn zài zǒu ba.
A. Búle, wǒ diànzhe jiālǐ de háizi ne.
B. Nā wǒ jiù bu liú nǐ le.

极 jí
Extremely.

再 zài
Then, only then.

惦 diàn
Be concerned about,
feel anxious.

留 liú
To detain, stay,
keep.

K. Cultural Notes

Apologies. Chinese tend to apologize for the same things
Westerners do: for doing something wrong and for inconveniencing
others. But there is a difference in the view of involuntary
physiological reactions by Chinese and Westerners. Westerners
tend to think that coughing, sneezing, yawning, hiccuping, and
belching are offensive to others. So they apologize. The Chinese don't think that there is anything wrong or offensive in
these involuntary reactions—and they don't apologize.

Traffic. There are no private cars in China—though very
important people always have access to a factory or government
car. Traffic consists mainly of buses, trolley buses, street
cars, subways, horse wagons, and bicycles. Bicycles are extremely common (most families have two or three). And bicycle parking
lots are a source of amazement to most Westerners: a veritable
sea of bicycles.

LESSON 5

REQUESTS AND WISHES

请 求 和 愿 望

A. Dialog: Pinyin Transcription

Tāngmǔ:	Wáng jiàoshòu,	1
	wǒ xiǎng qǐng nǐ bāng ge máng.	2
Wáng:	Shémme shì ya?	3
Tāngmǔ:	Wǒ xiǎng jìn yi bù tígāo Zhōngwén.	4
	Qǐng nǐ bāng wǒ zhǎo yiwèi jiātíng jiàoshī.	5
Wáng:	Hǎo a. Měi xīngqī xué jǐ cì ya?	6
Tāngmǔ:	Měi xīngqī sān cì, měi cì yī xiǎoshí.	7
Wáng:	Xíng.	8
	Wǒ zhǎo dào héshìde[1]	9
	jiù gěi nǐ dǎ diànhuà, hǎo ma?	10
Tāngmǔ:	Hǎo. Ē··· duìle, jǐ diǎnzhōng le?	11
Wáng:	Shí yī diǎn le.	12
Tāngmǔ:	Wǒ děi zǒule.	13
	Wǒ gāi zuò jǐlù gōnggòng qìchē huí qù ne?	14
Wáng:	Bié zháojí.	15
	Wǒ sòng nǐ dào chēzhàn.	16

B. DIALOG: SIMPLIFIED CHARACTERS

汤姆: 王教授，   1
       我想请你帮个忙。   2

王: 什么事呀？   3

汤姆: 我想进一步提高中文，   4
       请你帮我找一位家庭教师。   5

王: 好啊，每星期学几次呀？   6

汤姆: 每星期三次，每次一小时。   7

王: 行。   8
       我找到合适的[1]   9
       就给你打电话，好吗？   10

汤姆: 好。呃…对了。几点钟了？   11

王: 十一点了。   12

汤姆: 我得走了，   13
       我该坐几路公共汽车回去呢？   14

王: 别着急。   15
       我送你到车站。   16

C. Dialog: Yale Transcription

Tāngmǔ:	Wáng jyàushòu,	1
	wǒ syǎng chǐng nǐ bāng ge máng.	2
Wáng:	Shémme shr̀ ya?	3
Tāngmǔ:	Wǒ syǎng jìn yi bù tígāu Jūngwén.	4
	Chǐng nǐ bāng wǒ jǎu yiwèi jyātíng jyàushr̄.	5
Wáng:	Hǎu a. Měi syīngchī sywé jǐ tsz̀ ya?	6
Tāngmǔ:	Měi syīngchī sān tsz̀, měi tsz̀ yī syǎushŕ.	7
Wáng:	Syíng.	8
	Wǒ jǎu dàu héshr̀de[1]	9
	jyòu gěi nǐ dǎ dyànhwà, hǎu ma?	10
Tāngmǔ:	Hǎu. Ē··· dwèile, jǐ dyǎnjūng le?	11
Wáng:	Shŕ yī dyǎn le.	12
Tāngmǔ:	Wǒ děi dzǒule.	13
	Wǒ gāi dzwò jǐlù gūnggùng chìchē hwéi chyù ne?	14
Wáng:	Byé jáují.	15
	Wǒ sòng nǐ dàu chējàn.	16

D. DIALOG: FULL CHARACTERS

湯姆:	王教授，	1
	我想請你幫個忙。	2
王:	甚麼事呀？	3
湯姆:	我想進一步提高中文，	4
	請你幫我找一位家庭教師。	5
王:	好啊，每星期學幾次呀？	6
湯姆:	每星期三次，每次一小時。	7
王:	行。	8
	我找到合適的[1]	9
	就給你打電話，好嗎？	10
湯姆:	好。呃…對了。幾點鐘了？	11
王:	十一點了。	12
湯姆:	我得走了，	13
	我該坐幾路公共汽車回去呢？	14
王:	別着急。	15
	我送你到車站。	16

E. Dialog: Vocabulary and Notes

请求 qǐngqiú
To request.

愿望 yuànwàng
To wish, hope for.

帮 bāng
To help.

忙 máng
Busy, be busy.

帮忙 bāng máng
To help with the
thing one is busy
doing.

帮个忙 bāng ge máng
To do a favor.

进 jìn
To enter, advance.

进步 jìnbù
To progress, get
ahead, advance.

提高 tí gāo
To raise.

教师 jiàoshī
A teacher.

家庭教师 jiātíng jiàoshī
A private tutor.

星期 xīngqī
Week.

小时 xiǎoshí
Hour.

找到 zhǎo dào
To find (hunt and
get).

合适 héshì
To fit, be suitable.

该 gāi
Ought, should.

路 lù
Road, route.

几路公共汽车? What bus
number?

五路公共汽车 Bus route
number 5.

着急 zháojí
Worried, anxious.

送 sòng
To send, take some-
one somewhere.

车站 chē zhàn
Bus stop, bus or
train station.

1. héshìde.[a] The noun is dropped and the modifier becomes the
noun: a suitable *one*.

a. 合适的

F. Dialog: English

Tom:	Professor Wang,	1
	I'd like to ask you a favor.	2
Wang:	What is it?	3
Tom:	I'd like to improve my Chinese.	4
	Could you help me find a private tutor?	5
Wang:	Sure. How many times a week do you want to study?	6
Tom:	Three times a week, and one hour each time.	7
Wang:	O.K.	8
	When I find a suitable person,	9
	I'll phone you. Is that all right?	10
Tom:	Great. Uh··· by the way, what time is it?	11
Wang:	Eleven o'clock.	12
Tom:	I've got to go.	13
	What bus should I take to get home?	14
Wang:	Don't worry.	15
	I'll take you to the bus stop.	16

G. SUBSTITUTIONS: FULL CHARACTERS AND ENGLISH

1. 請進.
    　關門
    　開窗戶
    　隨手關燈
    　幫個忙
    　幫我找一位家庭教師

    Please come in.
    　　　close the door
    　　　open the window
    　　　turn off the light on your way out
    　　　do me a favor
    　　　help me find a private tutor

2. 我想請你幫個忙.
    　　帶些東西
    　　教我中文
    　　寫幾個中文字

    I wanted to ask you to help me (do me a favor).
    　　　　　　　take some things with you
    　　　　　　　teach me Chinese
    　　　　　　　write some Chinese characters

H. SUBSTITUTIONS: SIMPLIFIED CHARACTERS AND PINYIN

1.

请进，
关门
开窗户
随手关灯
帮个忙
帮我找一位家庭教师

Qǐng jìn.
guān mén
kāi chuāng·hù
suí shǒu guān dēng
bāng ge máng
bāng wǒ zhǎo yi wèi jiātíng jiàoshī

2.

我想请你帮个忙。
带些东西
教我中文
写几个中文字

Wǒ xiǎng qǐng nǐ bāng ge máng.
dàixiē dōngxi
jiāo wǒ Zhōngwén
xiě jǐ ge Zhōngwén zì

G (2)

3.
A. 每星期學幾次？	B. 每星期學三次。
次　　幾小時	次　　一小時

A. How many times a week?　B. Three times a week.
　　how many hours　time　　　　one hour　　　time

4.　我找到合適的就給你打電話。

　　　　好的

　　　　便宜的

　　　　最好的

When I find a suitable one, I'll phone you.
　　　　　　a good one
　　　　　　a cheap one
　　　　　　the best one

5.　別着急，我送你到車站。

　　　　我送你到飛機場

　　　　我幫你做

　　　　我有錢

Don't worry, I'll take you to the bus stop.
　　　　　　I'll take you to the airport
　　　　　　I'll help you do it
　　　　　　I've got some money

H (2)

3. A. 每星期学几次？　　B. 每星期学三次。
   　　次　　几小时　　　　　次　　　一小时

   A. Měi xīngqī xué jǐ cì?　　B. Měi xīngqī xué sān cì.
   　　cì　　jǐ xiǎoshí　　　　　cì　　　yī xiǎoshí

4. 我找到合适的就给你打电话。
   　　　　好的
   　　　　便宜的
   　　　　最好的

   Wǒ zhǎodào héshìde jiù gěi nǐ dǎ diànhuà.
   　　　　hǎo de
   　　　　pián·yìde
   　　　　zuì hǎo de

5. 别着急，我送你到车站。
   　　　　我送你到飞机场
   　　　　我帮你做
   　　　　我有钱

   Bié zháojí, wǒ sòng nǐ dào chēzhàn.
   　　　　wǒ sòng nǐ dào fēijī chǎng
   　　　　wǒ bāng nǐ zuò
   　　　　wǒ yǒu qián

I. Mini Dialogs: Full Characters and English

1.
A. 這兒能抽烟嗎？

B. 對不起。你可以在那兒抽。

A. Is it all right to smoke here?
B. Sorry. You can smoke over there.

2.
A. 對不起，我可以用你的字典嗎？

B. 啊呀，我正在用呢。

A. Excuse me, can I use your dictionary?
B. Oh, I'm sorry. I'm using it now.

3.
A. 這個東西中國話怎麼說的？

B. 中國話叫做自行車。

英文怎麼說的呢？

A. 英文叫做 bicycle.

A. What do you call this in Chinese?
B. It's called a zìxíngchē.
   What is it in English?
A. It's called a bicycle in English.

抽烟   chōu yān
        To smoke.

J. Mini Dialogs: Simplified Characters and Pinyin

1.
A. 这儿能抽烟吗？

B. 对不起，你可以在那儿抽。

A. Zhèr néng chōuyān ma?
B. Duìbuqǐ. Nǐ kěyǐ zài nàr chōu.

2.
A. 对不起，我可以用你的字典吗？

B. 啊呀，我正在用呢。

A. Duìbuqǐ, wǒ kěyǐ yòng nǐde zìdiǎn ma?
B. Āyà, wǒ zhèngzai yòng ne.

3.
A. 这个东西中国话怎么说的？

B. 中国话叫做自行车。

英文怎么说的呢？

A. 英文叫做 bicycle.

A. Zhèige dōngxi Zhōngguo huà zěmme shuō de?
B. Zhōngguo huà jiàozuo zìxíngchē.
Yīngwén zěmme shuō de ne?
A. Yīngwén jiàozuo bicycle.

正在   zhèng·zài   Just in the process of.   叫做   jiào·zuò   To be called.

I (2)

4.
A. 我可以借你的自行車嗎？

B. 可以。給你。

A. 今天晚上還給你。

B. 你一直用好了。没關係。

A. Can I borrow your bicycle?
  B. Sure. Here you are.
A. I'll get it back to you this evening.
  B. Keep it as long as you want. Don't worry about it.

5.
A. 請問現在幾點鐘了？

B. 五點了。

A. Could you tell me what time it is?
  B. Five o'clock.

6.
A. 我渴了。

B. 喝些茶，怎麽樣？

A. I'm thirsty.
  B. Why don't you have some tea?

借 jiè
To borrow or lend.

还 huán
To return something.

J (2)

4.
A. 我可以借你的自行车吗？

B. 可以。给你。

A. 今天晚上还给你。

B. 你一直用好了。没关系。

A. Wǒ kéyǐ jiè nǐde zìxíngchē ma?
B. Kéyǐ. Gěi nǐ.
A. Jīntiān wǎnshàng huán gěi nǐ.
B. Nǐ yìzhí yòng hǎole. Méi guānxi.

5.
A. 请问现在几点钟了？

B. 五点了。

A. Qǐng wèn, xiànzài jǐ diǎnzhōngle?
B. Wǔ diǎnle.

6.
A. 我渴了。

B. 喝些茶，怎么样？

A. Wǒ kěle.
B. Hē xiē chá, zěmme yàng?

一直　yìzhí
Straight through,
all the while.

渴　kě
Thirsty.

K. CULTURAL NOTES

Getting advice. There are two cultural points that sometimes combine to make an American uncomfortable when getting advice from a Chinese. 1) The American's desire for independence
(that is, doing your own thing in your own way) disposes him to
expect something more like 'I would ···' or 'If I were you ···'
when getting advice than 'You should ···'. And 2) Americans normally stay farther apart when talking to each other than the
Chinese do. This combination of the Chinese being much too
'close' and much too 'presumptuous' might tend to upset an American (without his consciously understanding why), when the Chinese is really just offering patient help, friendly advice, or
information.

LESSON 6

LEARNING CHINESE

学 中 文

A. DIALOG: PINYIN TRANSCRIPTION

Wáng: Tāngmǔ, hǎo jiǔ[1] bujiànle.   1

          Zài máng shémme ya?   2

Tāngmǔ: Āyà,[2] měitiān wǎnshàng zài mángzhe xué Zhōngwén ne.[3]   3

Wáng: Guàibude nǐde Zhōngwén jìnbù de nàme kuài.   4

Tāngmǔ: Ó, guòjiǎng guòjiǎng.   5

          Wǒ jiǎng ne, hái mámahuhū.   6

          kěshì dú hé xiě, wǒ hái hěn chà.   7

          Wǒ xiě de Zhōngwén xìn,   8

          Zhōngguo péngyou shuō kàn budǒng.   9

Wáng: Nǐ juéde Zhōngwén nán xué ma?   10

Tāngmǔ: Xué jiǎng Zhōngguo huà bu nán,   11

          kěshì dú hé xiě hěn nán.   12

Wáng: Jiùshì a.   13

Tāngmǔ: Kěshì wǒ háishì juéde xué Zhōngwén hěn yǒu yìsi.   14

          Wǒ hái dǎsuàn xué Zhōngguo shūfǎ ne.   15

          Zài wǒ xīnmù zhōng, Zhōngguo zì zuì piàoliang.   16

          Yuè kàn, yuè hǎokàn.   17

B. DIALOG: SIMPLIFIED CHARACTERS

王: 汤姆，好久[1]不见了，　　　　　　　　　　1
在忙什么呀？　　　　　　　　　　　　　　2

汤姆: 啊呀[2]，每天晚上在忙着学中文呢[3]。　　3

王: 怪不得你的中文进步得那么快。　　　　4

汤姆: 哦，过奖过奖。　　　　　　　　　　　　5
我讲呢，还马马虎虎，　　　　　　　　　6
可是读和写，我还很差。　　　　　　　7
我写的中文仗，　　　　　　　　　　　8
中国朋友说看不懂。　　　　　　　　　9

王: 你觉得中文难学吗？　　　　　　　　　10

汤姆: 学讲中国话不难，　　　　　　　　　　11
可是读和写很难。　　　　　　　　　　12

王: 就是啊。　　　　　　　　　　　　　　13

汤姆: 可是我还是觉得学中文很有意思。　　14
我还打算学中国书法呢。　　　　　　15
在我心目中中国字最漂亮，　　　　16
越看越好看。　　　　　　　　　　　　17

C. Dialog: Yale Transcription

Wáng:	Tāngmǔ, hǎu jyǒu[1] bujyànle.	1
	Dzài máng shémme ya?	2
Tāngmǔ:	Āyà,[2] měityān wǎnshàng dzài mángje sywé Jūngwén ne.[3]	3
Wáng:	Gwàibude nǐde Jūngwén jìnbù de nàme kwài.	4
Tāngmǔ:	Ó, gwòjyǎng gwòjyǎng.	5
	Wǒ jyǎng ne, hái mámahuhū.	6
	kěshr̀ dú hé syě, wǒ hái hěn chà.	7
	Wǒ syě de Jūngwén syìn,	8
	Jūnggwo péngyou shwō kàn budǔng.	9
Wáng:	Nǐ jywéde Jūngwén nán sywé ma?	10
Tāngmǔ:	Sywé jyǎng Jūnggwo hwà bu nán,	11
	kěshr̀ dú hé syě hěn nán.	12
Wáng:	Jyòushr̀ a.	13
Tāngmǔ:	Kěshr̀ wǒ háishr̀ jywéde sywé Jūngwén hěn yǒu yìsz.	14
	Wǒ hái dǎswàn sywé Jūnggwo shūfǎ ne.	15
	Dzài wǒ syīnmù jūng, Jūnggwo dz̀ dzwèi pyàulyang.	16
	Ywè kàn, ywè hǎukàn.	17

D. DIALOG: FULL CHARACTERS

王: 湯姆，好久[1]不見了，   1
　　　在忙甚麼呀？   2

湯姆: 啊呀[2]，每天晚上在忙着學中文呢[3]。   3

王: 怪不得你的中文進步得那麼快。   4

湯姆: 哦，過獎過獎。   5
　　　我講呢，還馬馬虎虎，   6
　　　可是讀和寫，我還很差。   7
　　　我寫的中文信，   8
　　　中國朋友說看不懂。   9

王: 你覺得中文難學嗎？   10

湯姆: 學講中國話不難，   11
　　　可是讀和寫很難。   12

王: 就是啊。   13

湯姆: 可是我還是覺得學中文很有意思。   14
　　　我還打算學中國書法呢。   15
　　　在我的心目中中國字最漂亮，   16
　　　越看越好看。   17

E. Dialog: Vocabulary and Notes

怪不得   guàibude
          No wonder.

还是   hái·shì
          Still.

过奖   guòjiǎng
          Excessive praise.
          (This is dropping
          out of use now.)

有意思   yǒu yì·sì
          Interesting.

打算   dǎsuàn
          To plan.

读   dú
          Read, study.

书法   shūfǎ
          Handwriting,
          calligraphy.

差   chà
          Poor, below
          standard.

心目中   xīnmù zhōng
          In one's mind's
          eye.

信   xìn
          A letter.

看不懂   kàn bu dǒng
          Read and not
          understand.

漂亮   piào·liàng
          Attractive, pretty,
          handsome.

觉得   jué·dé
          To feel.

越···越··· yuè ··· yuè ···
          The more ···,
          the more ····.

1. hǎo jiǔ.[a] A very long time. Hǎo[b] is used like hěn[c].

2. āyà.[d] Wang, with his reference to Tom's being busy, has im-
   plied that Tom is an important person. Tom uses this exclamation to modestly minimize the importance of what has
   been keeping him busy. 'Oh, it's no big deal.'

3. zài mángzhe xué Zhōngwén ne.[e] Continuous action is shown by
   any one, any two, or all three of the words zài, zhe, and ne.[f]

   a. 好久   c. 很   e. 在忙着学中文呢

   b. 好   d. 啊呀   f. 在 , 着 , 呢

F. Dialog: English

Wang:	I haven't seen you for a long time, Tom.	1
	What's been keeping you so busy?	2
Tom:	Oh, I've just been studying Chinese every night.	3
Wang:	No wonder your Chinese has been improving so fast.	4
Tom:	Oh, you're much too kind.	5
	My speaking is passable, I guess,	6
	but my reading and writing are still very poor.	7
	When I write letters in Chinese,	8
	my Chinese friends say they can't understand.	9
Wang:	Do you think Chinese is difficult?	10
Tom:	Learning to speak Chinese isn't so hard,	11
	but reading and writing are really tough.	12
Wang:	Exactly!	13
Tom:	But I still think Chinese is very interesting.	14
	And I'm still planning on studying Chinese calligraphy.	15
	I think Chinese characters are really beautiful.	16
	And the more you look at them, the prettier they get.	17

G. Substitutions: Full Characters and English

1. 在<u>吃</u>着呢。
    玩兒
    談話   (在談着話呢。)
    等你   (在等着你呢。)
    忙學中文   (在忙着學中文呢。)

   I'm <u>eating</u>.
       play
       talk
       wait for you
       busy studying Chinese

2. 在<u>忙</u>甚麼呀？
    幹
    買
   在<u>寫</u>甚麼<u>信</u>呀，
    賣   東西
    看   電影

   What are you <u>busy with</u>?
                doing
                buying
   What <u>letter</u> are you <u>writing</u>?
       things   selling
       movie   watching

H. SUBSTITUTIONS: SIMPLIFIED CHARACTERS AND PINYIN

---

1. 在吃着呢。

   玩儿

   谈话   (在谈着话呢。)

   等你   (在等着你呢。)

   忙学中文   (在忙着学中文呢。)

   Zài chī zhe ne.
       wǎr
       tán huà   (Zài tán zhe huà ne.)
       děng nǐ   (Zài děng zhe nǐ ne.)
       máng xué Zhōngwén (Zài máng zhe xué Zhōngwén ne.)

---

2. 在忙什么呀？

   干

   买

   在写什么仗呀？

   卖   东西

   看   电影

   Zài máng shémme ya?
       gàn
       mǎi
   Zài xiě shémme xìn ya?
       mài   dōngxi
       kàn   diànyǐng

G (2)

3. 越<u>看</u>越<u>好看</u> 。

   學   難

   吃 好吃

   説 生氣

The more you <u>look at it</u>, the <u>prettier it gets</u>.
        study it   harder it gets
        eat   better it tastes
        talk   madder you get

4. 我講還<u>馬馬虎虎</u> 。   差不多

     可以   不錯

  I speak only <u>so so</u>.   approximately right
            passably   quite good

5. 怪不得你的<u>中文進步得那麼快</u> 。

     英文説   慢

     中國話講   流利

No wonder <u>your Chinese has progressed</u> so <u>fast</u>.
      you speak English   slow
      you speak Chinese   fluently

H (2)

3. 越看越好看。
   　　学　　难
   　　吃　　好吃
   　　说　　生气

   Yuè kàn, yuè hǎo kàn.
   　　xué　　　nán
   　　chī　　　hǎo chī
   　　shuō　　shēngqì

---

4. 我讲还马马虎虎。　　　　　差不多
   　　　可以　　　　　　　　　不错

   Wǒ jiǎng hái mámahuhū.　　　chàbuduō
   　　　　　kěyǐ　　　　　　　　bú cuò

---

5. 怪不得你的中文进步得那么快。
   　　　　英文说　　　　　慢
   　　　　中国话讲　　　流利

   Guàibude nǐde Zhōngwén jìnbù de nàme kuài.
   　　　　Yīngwén shuō　　　　　màn
   　　　　Zhōngguo huà jiǎng　　liúlì

I. MINI DIALOGS: FULL CHARACTERS AND ENGLISH

1.
A. 你會講中國話嗎 ？
   B. 會一點兒 。
A. 在哪兒學的呀 ？
   B. 在美國學的 。

A. Can you speak Chinese?
  B. A little.
A. Where did you learn it?
  B. In America.

2.
A. 你的中國話講得真流利 ， 學多久了 ？
   B. 十年前學過一點兒 。
      現在又正在學呢 。

A. Your Chinese is really fluent. How long did you study?
  B. Ten years ago I studied a little.
     Now I'm studying it again.

3.
A. 你學了幾年中文了 ？
   B. 差不多四年了 ， 可是說得還不好 。

A. How many years did you study Chinese?
  B. Almost four years, but I still can't speak very well.

流利　liúlì
To be fluent.

多久　duō jiǔ
How long?

J. MINI DIALOGS: SIMPLIFIED CHARACTERS AND PINYIN

1.
A. 你会讲中国话吗？

　B. 会一点儿。

A. 在哪儿学的呀？

　B. 在美国学的。

A. Nǐ huì jiǎng Zhōngguo huà ma?
B. Huì yi diǎr.
A. Zài nǎr xuéde ya?
B. Zài Měiguo xuéde.

2.
A. 你的中国话讲得真流利，学多久了？

　B. 十年前学过一点儿。

现在又正在学呢。

A. Nǐde Zhōngguo huà jiǎngde zhēn liúlì. Xué duōjiǔle?
B. Shí nián qián xuéguo yi diǎr.
Xiànzài yòu zhèngzai xué ne.

3.
A. 你学了几年中文了？

　B. 差不多四年了，可是说得还不好。

A. Nǐ xuéle jǐ nián Zhōngwén le?
B. Chàbuduō sì nián le, kěshì shuō de hái buhǎo.

又　yòu
　　Again.

I (2)

4.
A. 中文難嗎 ?

B. 不太難 。

A. 我也想學 。

B. 好啊 ，我們一起學吧 。

A. Is Chinese hard?
  B. Not too hard.
A. I'm thinking of studying it too.
  B. Good, we can study it together.

5.
A. 好久不見了 ，到哪兒去了 ?

B. 到中國去了 。

A. 去幹甚麼了 ?

B. 去學中文了 。

A. I haven't seen you for ages.   Where have you been?
  B. I've been to China.
A. What did you go there for?
  B. To study Chinese.

6.
A. 我的中文不太好 ，請你說慢一點兒 。

B. 好好好 。

A. My Chinese isn't too good.   Please speak a little slower.
  B. O.K.

一起   yìqǐ
        Together.

干   gàn
      To do, manage.

J (2)

4.
A. 中文难吗？

B. 不太难。

A. 我也想学。

B. 好啊，我们一起学吧。

A. Zhōngwén nán ma?
B. Bu tài nán.
A. Wǒ yě xiǎng xué.
B. Hǎo a, women yiqǐ xué ba.

5.
A. 好久不见了，到哪儿去了？

B. 到中国去了。

A. 去干什么了？

B. 去学中文了。

A. Hǎo jiǔ bujiànle. Dào nǎr qùle?
B. Dào Zhōngguo qùle.
A. Qù gàn shémme le?
B. Qù xué Zhōngwén le.

6.
A. 我的中文不太好，请你说慢一点儿。

B. 好好好。

A. Wǒde Zhōngwén bu tài hǎo. Qǐng nǐ shuō màn yidiǎr.
B. Hao hao hao.

K. CULTURAL NOTES

Chinese 'dialects'. Chinese has eight main dialect types. Dialects of different types are far more different from each other than the word 'dialect' usually suggests. In fact, if they weren't spoken within the same country and didn't use the same non-phonetic system of writing (which indicates the sameness of words no matter how differently they are pronounced), they would clearly be called different languages. The eight dialect types are listed below together with rough estimates at percentages of number of speakers (in front) and the provinces where they are spoken (in parentheses). A schematic 'map' is also shown. A real map of China is shown on page 274 for comparison.

71%   1. Mandarin dialects.
      a. Northern (Hebei, Henan, Shandong, and Manchuria—now called Northeastern China).
      b. Northwestern (Shanxi, Shaanxi, and Gansu).
      c. Southwestern (Hubei, Sichuan, Yunnan, and Guizhou).
      d. Eastern (Anhui and Jiangsu).
9%   2. Wu dialects, like Shanghai (Zhejiang and Jiangsu).
2%   3. Northern Min dialects, like Fuchou (Fujian).
2%   4. Southern Min dialects, like Amoy, Swatow, and Hainan (Fujian, Guangdong, and Hainan island).
5%   5. Cantonese dialects (Guangdong and Guangxi).
4%   6. Hakka dialects (Guangdong, Guangxi, Hunan, and Jiangxi).
5%   7. Xiang dialects (Hunan).
2%   8. Gan dialects (Jiangxi).

The different dialect types are at least as different from each other as are the Romance languages (French, Italian, Spanish, Portuguese, etc.), and at most as different as are the Germanic languages (English, Dutch, German, the Scandinavian languages, etc.). The sub-dialects within any type can be as different from each other as are the Scandinavian languages (Danish, Swedish, Norwegian, etc.).

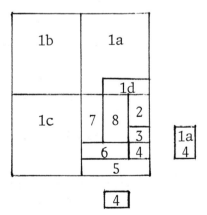

LESSON 7

SEEING A DOCTOR

看 病

A. Dialog: Pinyin Transcription

Ānnā:	Yīsheng, wǒ juéde bu shūfu.	1
Yīsheng:	Nǐ zěmme bu shūfu ya?	2
Ānnā:	Zuótiān wǒ kāishǐ liú bíti.	3
	Xiànzài juéde tóu téng.	4
Yīsheng:	Hóulong téng ma?	5
Ānnā:	Téng, hái fāshāo ne.	6
Yīsheng:	Duì, xiànzài nǐde tǐwēn shì sānshibā dù.	7
Ānnā:	Yīsheng, shémme bìng?	8
Yīsheng:	Gǎnmào.	9
Ānnā:	Yào dǎzhēn ma?	10
Yīsheng:	Bu dǎ, chī diǎr yào, xiūxi xiūxi.	11
	Guò jǐ tiān jiù hǎole.	12
	Zhèi shì chǔfāng.	13
Ānnā:	Hǎo. Xièxie.	14
Yīsheng:	Bu xiè.	15

B. DIALOG: SIMPLIFIED CHARACTERS

安娜: 医生，我觉得不舒服。 1

医生: 你怎么不舒服呀？ 2

安娜: 昨天我开始流鼻涕， 3
现在觉得头疼。 4

医生: 喉咙疼吗？ 5

安娜: 疼，还发烧呢。 6

医生: 对，现在你的体温是38度。 7

安娜: 医生，什么病？ 8

医生: 感冒。 9

安娜: 要打针吗？ 10

医生: 不打，吃点儿药，休息休息。 11
过几天就好了。 12
这是处方。 13

安娜: 好，谢谢。 14

医生: 不谢。 15

C. Dialog: Yale Transcription

Ānnā:	Yīsheng, wǒ jywéde bu shūfu.	1
Yīsheng:	Nǐ dzěmme bu shūfu ya?	2
Ānnā:	Dzwótyān wǒ kāishř lyóu bíti.	3
	Syàndzài jywéde tóu téng.	4
Yīsheng:	Hóulung téng ma?	5
Ānnā:	Téng, hái fāshāu ne.	6
Yīsheng:	Dwèi, syàndzài nǐde tǐwēn shř sānshrbā dù.	7
Ānnā:	Yīsheng, shémme bìng?	8
Yīsheng:	Gǎnmàu.	9
Ānnā:	Yàu dǎjēn ma?	10
Yīsheng:	Bu dǎ, chř dyǎr yàu, syōusyi syōusyi.	11
	Gwò jǐ tyān jyòu hǎule.	12
	Jèi shř chǔfāng.	13
Ānnā:	Hǎu. Syèsye.	14
Yīsheng:	Bu syè.	15

D. DIALOG: FULL CHARACTERS

安娜： 醫生，我覺得不舒服。   1

醫生： 你怎麼不舒服呀？   2

安娜： 昨天我開始流鼻涕，   3
　　　 現在覺得頭疼。   4

醫生： 喉嚨疼嗎？   5

安娜： 疼，還發燒呢。   6

醫生： 對，現在你的体溫是38度。   7

安娜： 醫生，甚麼病？   8

醫生： 感冒。   9

安娜： 要打針嗎？   10

醫生： 不打，吃點兒藥，休息休息，   11
　　　 過幾天就好了。   12
　　　 這是處方。   13

安娜： 好，謝謝。   14

醫生： 不謝。   15

E. Dialog: Vocabulary and Notes

病 bìng
Illness, sickness.

看病 kàn bìng
To see a doctor,
attend sickness,
diagnose a disease.

舒服 shū·fú
To feel well,
be comfortable.

开始 kāishǐ
To begin, start.

流 liú
To flow.

鼻 bí
Nose.

鼻涕 bí·tì
Mucus.

疼 téng
To ache, pain.

头疼 tóu téng
To have a headache.

喉咙 hóu·lóng
throat.

还 hái
And furthermore,
still, yet.

发烧 fāshāo
To have a tem-
perature.

体温 tǐwēn
Body temperature.

度 dù
A degree of tem-
perature or of an
angle.

感冒 gǎnmào
A cold, the flu.

针 zhēn
A needle.

打针 dǎzhēn
To give a shot.

药 yào
Medicine.

休息 xiū·xí
To rest.

过几天 guò jǐ tiān
To pass several
days, after sever-
al days.

处方 chùfāng
A prescription.

F. Dialog: English

Anna:	I don't feel very well, Doctor.	1
Doctor:	What's the matter?	2
Anna:	Yesterday my nose started to run.	3
	And now I've got a headache.	4
Doctor:	Have you got a sore throat?	5
Anna:	Yes, and I've also got a fever.	6
Doctor:	Yes, I see. Your temperature is 38 degrees (100.4).	7
Anna:	What have I got, Doctor?	8
Doctor:	A cold.	9
Anna:	Do I have to have a shot?	10
Doctor:	No. Just take some medicine and rest.	11
	After a few days, you'll be all right.	12
	Here's a prescription.	13
Anna:	O.K. Thanks.	14
Doctor:	You're welcome.	15

G. Substitutions: Full Characters and English

1.   頭疼嗎 ?   喉嚨
     牙   肚子
     背   耳朵

     Does your <u>head</u> ache?   throat
               tooth   belly
               back   ear

2.   昨天我開始流鼻涕。
           打噴嚏
           流眼淚
           發燒

     Yesterday <u>my nose started to run.</u>
               I started to sneeze
               my eyes started to run
               I started to have a fever

3.   現在我覺得頭疼
           不舒服
           喉嚨疼

     Now I feel <u>a headache</u>. (I've got a headache.)
                uncomfortable. (I don't feel well.)
                a sore throat. (I've got a sore throat.)

H. Substitutions: Simplified Characters and Pinyin

1.
头 疼 吗 ?   喉咙
牙   肚子
背   耳朵

Tóu téng ma?   hóu•lóng
yá   dùzi
bèi   ěr•duǒ

2.
昨天我开始流鼻涕。
打喷嚏
流眼泪
发烧

Zuótiān wǒ kāishǐ liú bí•tì.
dǎ pèn•tì
liú yǎnlèi
fāshāo

3.
现在我觉得头疼.
不舒服
喉咙疼

Xiànzài wǒ juéde tóu téng.
bu shū•fú
hóu•lóng téng

G (2)

4. 頭疼　還　發燒。
流鼻涕　　喉嚨疼
打噴嚏　　流眼淚

I've got a headache, and on top of that I've got a fever.
My nose is running   I've got a sore throat
I keep sneezing   my eyes are running

5. 你的體溫是 38 度。
　　體重　56 公斤
　　身高　　1 米 6

Your (body) temperature is 38 degrees C. (100.4° F.)
     (body) weight   56 kilograms (123 lbs.)
     (body) height   1.6 meters (5 foot 3)

6. A. 甚麼病？ B. 感冒。
　　　　　　　　　高血壓
　　　　　　　　　心臟病
　　　　　　　　　肺炎

A. What illness have I got? B. A cold.
                                high blood pressure
                                heart trouble
                                pneumonia

H (2)

4.
　　<u>头疼</u>，还　　<u>发烧</u>。
　　流鼻涕　　　喉咙疼
　　打喷嚏　　　流眼泪

　　<u>Tóu téng</u>,　hái　<u>fāshāo</u>.
　　liú bí‧tì　　　hóu‧lóng téng
　　dǎ pèn‧tì　　　liú yǎnlèi

5.
　　<u>你的体温是</u> <u>38 度</u>。
　　　　体重　　56 公斤
　　　　身高　　1 米 6

　　Nǐde <u>tǐwēn</u>　shì　<u>sānshibā dù</u>.
　　　　tǐzhòng　　　wǔshiliù gōng jīn
　　　　shēn-gāo　　yī mǐ liù

6.
　　A. 什么病?　　B. <u>感冒</u>。
　　　　　　　　　　高血压
　　　　　　　　　　心脏病
　　　　　　　　　　肺炎

　　A. Shémme bìng?　B. <u>Gǎnmào</u>.
　　　　　　　　　　　gāo xuèyā
　　　　　　　　　　　xīnzàng bìng
　　　　　　　　　　　fèiyán

I. Mini Dialogs: Full Characters and English

1. A. 大夫，我牙疼。
   B. 嗯，有一顆壞牙，
   得拔了。

A. Doctor, I've got a toothache.
B. Hmm, you've got a bad tooth.
It'll have to be pulled.

2. A. 我怕拔牙．疼嗎？
   B. 不太疼，我給你用
   針刺麻醉，好不好？
   A. 啊呀，我更害怕了。

A. I'm afraid of having a tooth pulled. Will it hurt?
B. Not too much. I can give you
acupuncture anesthesia if you want.
A. Oh no! I'm even more afraid of that.

牙	yá Tooth.	嘴	zuǐ Mouth.
拔	bá To pull out.	怕	pà To fear.
害怕	hàipà To fear.	好象	hǎoxiàng Just like.
心脏	xīn zàng The heart.	心脏病	xīn zàng bìng Heart trouble.

J. Mini Dialogs: Simplified Characters and Pinyin

1.
A. 大夫，我牙疼。
B. 姆，有一颗坏牙。
得拔了。

A. Dàifu, wǒ yá téng.
B. Mmm, yǒu yi kē huài yá.
Děi bále.

2.
A. 我怕拔牙。疼吗？
B. 不太疼，我给你用
针刺麻醉，好不好？
A. 啊呀，我更害怕了。

A. Wǒ pà bá yá. Téng ma?
B. Bu tài téng. Wǒ gěi nǐ yòng
zhēncì mázuì, hǎo bu hǎo?
A. Āyà, wǒ gèng hàipàle.

张嘴	zhāng zuǐ To open the mouth.	颗	kē Classifier of teeth.
麻醉	mázuì Anesthesia.	针刺麻醉	zhēncì mázuì Acupuncture anesthesia.
肚子	dùzi Stomach or belly.	检查	jiǎnchá To examine.
头晕	tóuyùn To be dizzy.	血压	xuèyā Blood pressure.

I (2)

3.
A. 你好象病了。怎麽了？

B. 我肚子疼。

A. 你得去看醫生呀！

A. You look sick. What's the matter?
  B. I've got a stomach ache.
A. You should go see a doctor.

4.
A. 醫生，我覺得不舒服。

B. 我給你檢查一下。

A. 甚麽病？

B. 心臟病。

A. I don't feel very well, Doctor.
  B. I'll have to make some tests.
A. What have I got?
  B. Heart trouble.

5.
A. 大夫，我覺得頭暈。

B. 你的血壓很高。

A. 唉，真糟糕。

A. I feel dizzy, Doctor.
  B. You've got high blood pressure.
A. Gee, what rotten luck.

J (2)

3.
A. 你好象病了，怎么了？

　B. 我肚子疼。

A. 你得去看医生呀！

A. Nǐ hǎoxiàng bìngle. Zěmmele?
　B. Wǒ dùzi téng.
A. Nǐ děi qù kàn yīsheng ya!

4.
A. 医生，我觉得不舒服。

　B. 我给你检查一下。

A. 什么病？

　B. 心脏病。

A. Yīsheng, wǒ juéde bu shūfu.
　B. Wǒ gěi nǐ jiǎnchá yixià.
A. Shémme bìng?
　B. Xīnzàng bìng.

5.
A. 大夫，我觉得头晕。

　B. 你的血压很高。

A. 唉，真糟糕。

A. Dàifu, wǒ juéde tóuyùn.
　B. Nǐde xuèyā hěn gāo.
A. Hai, zhēn zāogāo.

K. Cultural Notes

Traditional Chinese medicine. The medicine practiced in
China today is a combination of Western medicine and traditional
Chinese medicine. The proportions vary from mostly Western to
mostly Chinese, but there is usually some degree of mixture. The
main distinguishing features of traditional Chinese medicine are
the following. 1) A wide variety of herbs used as medicines.
2) Pneumotherapy (controlled breathing). 3) Bone-setting.
4) Moxibustion (the burning of aromatic herbs at crucial points
of the body, often in connection with acupuncture). 5) Acupuncture. This last point has attracted more interest throughout the
world than the others and a brief description is given here.

Acupuncture is basically a method of stimulating special
points in the nervous system (xuè wèi[a]). (As a start, it may
help to think of acupuncture doing for nerves what massage does
for muscles—but this comparison should not be pressed too far.)
A needle is used to penetrate the skin and muscle and make con-
tact with the desired point. The needle is then manipulated so
as to bring about the stimulation. This manipulation is now done
with an electrical apparatus that vibrates the needle, but in
earlier times it was done by manual twirling or rotating of the
needle. Acupuncture can be used either to treat ailments (like
headaches or gallstones) or to anesthetize. Acupuncture anesthesia is commonly used along with dental work and with Western
surgery in areas of the head, neck, and lower abdomen.

a. 穴位

LESSON 8

GREETINGS

问　候

A. Dialog: Pinyin Transcription

Tāngmǔ: Hài,[1] Wáng jiàoshòu.   1

Wáng: Hài, Tāngmǔ. Nǐ hǎo?   2

Tāngmǔ: Hǎo a. Nǐ ne? Zuìjìn zěmme yàng?   3

Wáng: Hai, lǎo yàngzi.   4
         Tīngshuō nǐ tàitai bìngle. Hǎole ma?   5

Tāngmǔ: Hǎole.   6

Wáng: Xiàng tā wèn hǎo.   7

Tāngmǔ: Hǎo. Nǐ quánjiā dōu hǎo ma?   8

Wáng: Tāmen dōu hěn hǎo. Xièxie nǐ.   9
         Nǐ xiànzài hái nàme máng ma?   10

Tāngmǔ: Máng. Kěshì wǒ zìjǐ yě bu zhīdào zài[2] máng shémme.   11

Wáng: Bié tài lèile.   12

Tāngmǔ: Jiùshì a. Ò, wǒde gōnggòng qìchē láile.   13
         Yǒu biàn dào wǒ jiā lái zuò yi zuo liáoliao ba.   14

Wáng: Hao hao hao.   15

B. Dialog: Simplified Characters

汤姆: 嗨¹，王教授。   1

王: 嗨，汤姆，你好？   2

汤姆: 好啊。你呢？最近怎么样？   3

王: 嘿，老样子。   4
　　听说你太太病了。好了吗？   5

汤姆: 好了。   6

王: 向她问好。   7

汤姆: 好。你全家都好吗？   8

王: 他们都很好。谢谢你。   9
　　你现在还那么忙吗？   10

汤姆: 忙。可是我自己也不知道在²忙什么。   11

王: 别太累了。   12

汤姆: 就是啊。喔，我的公共汽车来了。   13
　　有便到我家来坐一坐聊聊吧。   14

王: 好好好。   15

C. DIALOG: YALE TRANSCRIPTION

Tāngmǔ: Hài,[1] Wáng jyàushòu.   1

Wáng: Hài, Tāngmǔ. Nǐ hǎu?   2

Tāngmǔ: Hǎu a. Nǐ ne? Dzwèi jìn dzěmme yàng?   3

Wáng: Hai, lǎu yàngdz.   4
         Tīngshwō nǐ tàitai bìngle. Hǎule ma?   5

Tāngmǔ: Hǎule.   6

Wáng: Syàng tā wèn hǎu.   7

Tāngmǔ: Hǎu. Nǐ chywánjyā dōu hǎu ma?   8

Wáng: Tāmen dōu hěn hǎu. Syèsye nǐ.   9
         Nǐ syàndzài hái nàme máng ma?   10

Tāngmǔ: Máng. Kěshr̀ wǒ dz̀jǐ yě bu jr̄dàu dzài[2] máng shémme.   11

Wáng: Bié tài lèile.   12

Tāngmǔ: Jyòushr̀ a. Ò, wǒde gūnggùng chìchē láile.   13
         Yǒu byàn dàu wǒ jyā lái dzwò yi dzwo lyáulyau ba.   14

Wáng: Hau hau hau.   15

D. Dialog: Full Characters

湯姆: 嗨[1]，王教授。　　　　　　　　　1

王: 嗨，湯姆，你好？　　　　　　　　2

湯姆: 好啊。你呢？最近怎麼樣？　　　3

王: 嘿，老樣子。　　　　　　　　　　4
聽說你太太病了。好了嗎？　　5

湯姆: 好了。　　　　　　　　　　　　　6

王: 向她問好。　　　　　　　　　　　7

湯姆: 好。你全家都好嗎？　　　　　　8

王: 他們都很好。謝謝你。　　　　　9
你現在還那麼忙嗎？　　　　　10

湯姆: 忙。可是我自己也不知道在[2]忙甚麼。　11

王: 別太累了。　　　　　　　　　　　12

湯姆: 就是啊。喔，我的公共汽車來了。　13
有便到我家來坐一坐聊聊吧。　14

王: 好好好。　　　　　　　　　　　　15

E. Dialog: Vocabulary and Notes.

问候
wènhòu
Greetings; to in-
quire after, send
regrets.

问好
wèn hǎo
To ask after the
health of another.

最近
zuìjìn
Recently, in the
near future.

全家
quán jiā
The whole family.

老样子
lǎo yàngzi
Same as usual.

累
lèi
To be tired.

听说
tīngshuō
To hear it said that.

有便
yǒu biàn
To be convenient
(have convenience).

向
xiàng
To, towards.

聊
liáo
To chat.

1. <u>hài</u>.[a] This is used to call out to someone with a pleasant
   feeling: 'Oh, how nice!'

2. This is the continuous use of <u>zài</u>.[b]
   'What I'm being busy with.'

   a. 嗨   b. 在

F. Dialog: English

Tom:	Ah, Professor Wang.	1
Wang:	Oh! Tom. How are you?	2
Tom:	Fine. And you? How have you been lately?	3
Wang:	Oh ··· same as usual.	4
	I hear your wife was sick. Is she all right now?	5
Tom:	Yes, she's fine.	6
Wang:	Give her my regards.	7
Tom:	O.K. Is your whole family well?	8
Wang:	Yes they are, thanks.	9
	Are you still as busy as ever?	10
Tom:	Yes, but even I don't know what I'm so busy with.	11
Wang:	Don't tire yourself out too much.	12
Tom:	I won't. Oh, here comes my bus.	13
	Come over and sit and talk when you get a chance.	14
Wang:	O.K.	15

G. SUBSTITUTIONS: FULL CHARACTERS AND ENGLISH

1. | 嘿，老樣子.   就那樣
   | 還可以   還過得去

   Oh, the same as usual.   so so
       passable   still getting by

2. | 最近怎麼樣?
   | 好嗎
   | 身體好嗎
   | 忙嗎

   How have you been lately?
   have you been well
   have you been in good shape
   have you been busy

3. | 有便,   到我家來坐一坐聊聊.
   | 空   吃飯
   | 工夫   玩兒
   | 時間   喝杯茶談談

   When it's convenient, come to my house to sit and chat.
       you are free   to eat
       you have some leisure time   to have some fun
       you have some time   for tea and a chat

H. Substitutions: Simplified Characters and Pinyin

1.	嘿，老样子。	就那样
	还可以	还过得去

Hai, <u>lǎo yàngzi</u>.   jiù nèi yàng
    hái kéyǐ   hái guò de qù

2.	最近怎么样?
	好吗
	身体好吗
	忙吗

Zuìjìn <u>zěmme yàng</u>?
    hǎo ma
    shēn·tǐ hǎo ma
    máng ma

3.	有便, 到我家来坐一坐聊聊。	
	空	吃饭
	工夫	玩儿
	时间	喝杯茶谈谈

Yǒu <u>biàn</u>,   dào wǒ jiā lái <u>zuò yi zuò liáoliao</u>.
    kòng   chī fàn
    gōng·fū   wǎr
    shíjiān   hē bēi chá tántan

I. Mini Dialogs: Full Characters and English

1.
A. 你到哪兒去呀？
   B. 上課去，你呢？
A. 吃飯去。

A. Where are you going?
   B. To class. And you?
A. I'm going to get something to eat.

2.
A. 吃飯了嗎？
   B. 吃了，你吃了嗎？
A. 還沒呢。

A. Have you eaten yet?
   B. Yes. Have you?
A. I haven't.

3.
A. 嗨，最近在忙甚麼呀？
   B. 在忙考試呢。
A. 祝你成功。

A. Hey! What's been keeping you so busy lately?
   B. I've been busy preparing for a test.
A. Good luck!

課 kè
    Lessons, class.

考试 kǎoshì
      Test, to test.

J. MINI DIALOGS: SIMPLIFIED CHARACTERS AND PINYIN

1.
> A. 你到哪儿去呀?
>
> B. 上课去，你呢?
>
> A. 吃饭去。
>
> A. Nǐ dào nǎr qù ya?
> B. Shàng kè qù. Nǐ ne?
> A. Chī fàn qù.

2.
> A. 吃饭了吗?
>
> B. 吃了。你吃了吗?
>
> A. 还没呢。
>
> A. Chī fànle ma?
> B. Chīle. Nǐ chīle ma?
> A. Hái méi ne.

3.
> A. 嗨，最近在忙什么呀?
>
> B. 在忙考试呢。
>
> A. 祝你成功。
>
> A. Hài, zuìjìn zài máng shémme ya?
> B. Zài máng kǎo shì ne.
> A. Zhù nǐ chénggōng.

祝 zhù
To wish someone something.

成功 chénggōng
Success, to succeed.

I (2)

4.
> A. 老大爺（老大娘），
>
>   最近身體怎麼樣？
>
> B. 很好，托您的福。

> A. 'Grandfather' ('grandmother').
>   How has your health been recently?
> B. Fine, thanks to you.

5.
> A. 嗨，好久不見了，
>
>   你一直在哪兒呀？
>
>   在忙着談戀愛吧？
>
> B. 別瞎說了。
>
> A. 好吧，祝你幸福。

> A. Hey, I haven't seen you for a long time.
>   Where have you been all this time?
>   Have you been busy courting?
> B. Don't be silly.
> A. O.K. But good luck (in your coming marriage).

大爺	dà yé Term of respect for an old man.	大娘	dà niáng Term of respect for an old lady.
托您的福	tuō nínde fú Thanks to you.	戀愛	liàn ài Love between sweethearts.
瞎說	xiā shuō To talk nonsense.		

J (2)

4.
A. 老大爷（老大娘），
   最近身体怎么样？
B. 很好，托您的福。

A. Lǎo dà yé (lǎo dà niáng).
   Zuìjìn shēnti zěmme yàng?
B. Hěn hǎo, tuō nínde fú.

5.
A. 嗨，好久不见了，
   你一直在哪儿呀？
   在忙着谈恋爱吧？
B. 别瞎说了。
A. 好吧，祝你幸福。

A. Hài, hǎo jiǔ bu jiànle.
   Nǐ yìzhí zài nǎr ya?
   Zài mángzhe tán liàn ài ba?
B. Bié xiā shuōle.
A. Hǎo ba, zhù nǐ xìngfú.

身体	shēn•tǐ Body.	托福	tuō fú Thanks to.
谈恋爱	tán liàn ài To court, woo.	瞎	xiā To be blind, blindly, nonsensically, muddled.
幸福	xìngfú To be happy (especially in marriage).		

K. Cultural Notes

The main greetings in English (except for the meaningless 'Hello' and 'Hi') are concerned with a person's health. Questions like 'How are you?' are asked, and simple answers like 'Fine' are given. The questioner is not really interested in how you are, and true details in the answer would be boring.

In addition to questions about a person's health, Chinese greetings can also ask about where a person is going, whether he has eaten yet, and how busy he has been. And short, noncommittal answers (not true, boring details) are all that the questioner usually expects. Some topics are more common at some levels of society and age than others, however. Here is a rough guide. Each example has many variations.

你吃了吗？	Nǐ chīle ma? Have you eaten?	Used by people at all levels. For farmers, these are
你到哪儿去？	Nǐ dào nǎr qù? Where're you going?	the main greetings.
你好啊？	Nǐ hǎo a? How are you?	Used by city people, not farmers.
你忙吗？	Nǐ máng ma? Are you busy?	Used by intellectuals, office workers, and the
最近怎么样？	Zuìjìn zěmme yàng? How have things been?	like.
最近身体怎么样？	Zuìjìn shēnti zěmme yàng? Have you been well?	Used to elderly people.

Respect for age. The big difference between the Chinese and Western attitude towards old age is shown by the difficulty of finding English equivalents for lǎo dà yé and lǎo dà niáng (see mini dialog 4). When respectfully addressing an old person in English, one avoids any mention of old age. To call an old man 'Grandpa' in English tends to show less respect than a neutral term like 'Mister' or 'Sir'. But in Chinese, an equivalent term would show greater respect.

LESSON 9

INVITATIONS

邀 请

A. Dialog: Pinyin Transcription

Wáng:	Tāngmǔ, nǐ hé nǐ tàitai	1
	zhèige xīngqī[1] liù wǎnshàng yǒu kòng ma?	2
Tāngmǔ:	Yǒu kòng. Shémme shì ya?	3
Wáng:	Wǒ xiǎng qǐng nǐmen liǎng wèi dào wǒ jiā qù	4
	chī Zhōngguo fàn.	5
Tāngmǔ:	Tài hǎole, wǒmen xǐhuān chī Zhōngguo fàn.	6
	Zhōngguo fàn zài Měiguo shì yǒu míng de.	7
	Duìle, yǒu shémme tèbié de shì qǐng kè ma?	8
Wáng:	Méi yǒu shémme tèbié de shì.	9
Tāngmǔ:	Hái yǒu bié de kèrén ma?	10
Wáng:	Méi yǒu, jiù wǒmen liǎng jiā,	11
	zhōumò zài yiqǐ zuò yizuo liáoliao tiān.	12
Tāngmǔ:	Hǎo jíle.	13
Wáng:	Nàme xīngqī liù wǎnshàng qī diǎnzhōng	14
	yidìng lái ba.	15
Tāngmǔ:	yídìng yidìng.	16

B. Dialog: Simplified Characters

王：　　汤姆，你和你太太　　　　　　　　　1
　　　　这个星期六晚上有空吗？　　　　　　2

汤姆：　有空，什么事呀？　　　　　　　　　3

王：　　我想请你们两位到我家去　　　　　　4
　　　　吃中国饭。　　　　　　　　　　　　5

汤姆：　太好了，我们喜欢吃中国饭，　　　　6
　　　　中国饭在美国是有名的。　　　　　　7
　　　　对了，有什么特别的事请客吗？　　　8

王：　　没有什么特别的事。　　　　　　　　9

汤姆：　还有别的客人吗？　　　　　　　　　10

王：　　没有，就我们两家，　　　　　　　　11
　　　　周末在一起坐一坐聊聊天。　　　　　12

汤姆：　好极了。　　　　　　　　　　　　　13

王：　　那么星期六晚上七点钟　　　　　　　14
　　　　一定来吧。　　　　　　　　　　　　15

汤姆：　一定、一定。　　　　　　　　　　　16

C. Dialog: Yale Transcription

Wáng:	Tāngmǔ, nǐ hé nǐ tàitai	1
	jèige syīngchī[1] lyòu wǎnshàng yǒu kùng ma?	2
Tāngmǔ:	Yǒu kùng. Shémme shr̀ ya?	3
Wáng:	Wǒ syǎng chǐng nǐmen lyǎng wèi dàu wǒ jyā chyù	4
	chr̄ Jūnggwo fàn.	5
Tāngmǔ:	Tài hǎule, wǒmen syīhwān chr̄ Jūnggwo fàn.	6
	Jūnggwo fàn dzài Měigwo shr̀ yǒu míng de.	7
	Dwèile, yǒu shémme tèbyé de shr̀ chǐng kè ma?	8
Wáng:	Méi yǒu shémme tèbyé de shr̀.	9
Tāngmǔ:	Hái yǒu byé de kèrén ma?	10
Wáng:	Méi yǒu, jyòu wǒmen lyǎng jyā,	11
	jōumwò dzài yichǐ dzwò yidzwo lyáulyau tyān.	12
Tāngmǔ:	Hǎu jíle.	13
Wáng:	Nàme syīngchī lyòu wǎnshàng chī dyǎnjūng	14
	yidìng lái ba.	15
Tāngmǔ:	Yídìng yidìng.	16

D. Dialog: Full Characters

王: 湯姆，你和你太太
這個星期六晚上有空嗎？ 1
2

湯姆: 有空，甚麼事呀？ 3

王: 我想請你們兩位到我家去
吃中國飯。 4
5

湯姆: 太好了，我們喜歡吃中國飯。
中國飯在美國是有名的。
對了，有甚麼特別的事請客嗎？ 6
7
8

王: 沒有甚麼特別的事。 9

湯姆: 還有別的客人嗎？ 10

王: 沒有，就我們兩家，
週末在一起坐一坐聊聊天。 11
12

湯姆: 好極了。 13

王: 那麼星期六晚上七點鐘
一定來吧。 14
15

湯姆: 一定、一定。 16

E. Dialog: Vocabulary and Notes

邀请　yāoqǐng
To invite.

什么事?　shémme shì
What affair or
business?

喜欢　xǐhuān
To like, feel
pleasure.

有名　yǒu míng
To be famous, be
prominent.

特别　tèbié
Special, distinc-
tive; especially.

请客　qǐngkè
To invite guests,
have a party.

客人　kèrén
Guests.

就　jiù
Only.

周　zhōu
A week (a round
or circuit).

末　mò
The end, last.

周末　zhōumò
Weekend.

聊聊天　liáoliao tiān
To pass the time
of day; chat.

一定　yídìng
For sure, cer-
tainly.

1. Xīngqī[a] (literally, 'star' period) is much more commonly used
   for 'week' in modern China than lǐbài (worship), which arose
   from the Christian tradition of Sunday worship.

   a. 星期

F. Dialog: English

Wang:	Tom, are you and your wife	1
	going to be free this Saturday evening?	2
Tom:	Yes, we are. Why do you ask?	3
Wang:	I'd like to invite the two of you to our house	4
	for Chinese food.	5
Tom:	Oh, how nice. We love Chinese food.	6
	It's very well known in America.	7
	By the way, is it some special occasion?	8
Wang:	No, nothing special.	9
Tom:	Will there be any other guests?	10
Wang:	No. Just our two families	11
	getting together on a weekend to sit and chat.	12
Tom:	Excellent!	13
Wang:	O.K. then. Saturday night at 7 o'clock.	14
	Be sure to come.	15
Tom:	Oh, we will. We certainly will.	16

G. Substitutions: Full Characters and English

1. 這個星期六晚上　有空嗎？
   明天上午　　　　方便
   下星期日　　　　有時間

   <u>Are you free</u>　　<u>this Saturday night?</u>
   is it convenient　tomorrow morning
   do you have time　next Sunday

2. 我想請<u>你們兩位</u>　到我家去<u>吃中國飯</u>。
   　　　你們一家子　　　　　吃飯
   　　　你和你太太　　　　　吃日本飯

   I want to invite <u>the two of you</u> to my house <u>for Chinese food</u>.
   　　　　　　　　your family　　　　　　　 for dinner
   　　　　　　　　you and your wife　　　　　for Japanese food

3. <u>週末</u>在一起<u>坐一坐</u>聊聊天。
   新年　　　談談
   中秋節　　聚聚

   (a chance to) <u>chat</u> together <u>during the weekend.</u>
   　　　　　　　talk　　　　　　 during the New Year holiday
   　　　　　　　meet　　　　　　 during the Mid-Autumn Festival

H. SUBSTITUTIONS: SIMPLIFIED CHARACTERS AND PINYIN

1. 这个星期六晚上   有空吗?
   明天上午   方便
   下星期日   有时间

   Zhèige xīngqī liù wǎn·shàng   yǒu kòng ma?
   míngtiān shàngwǔ   fāngbian
   xià xīngqī rì   yǒu shíjiān

2. 我想请你们两位   到我家去 吃中国饭。
        你们一家子   吃饭
        你和你太太   吃日本饭

   Wǒ xiǎng qǐng nǐmen liǎngwèi dào wǒ jiā qù chī Zhōngguo fàn.
                 nǐmen yi jiāzi   chī fàn
                 nǐ hé nǐ tàitai   chī rìběn fàn

3. 周末   在一起坐一坐聊聊天 。
   新年   谈谈
   中秋节   聚聚

   Zhōumò   zài yiqǐ zuò yi zuo liáoliao tiān.
   xīn nián   tántan
   zhōngqiú jié   jùju

I. MINI DIALOGS: FULL CHARACTERS AND ENGLISH

1.
A. 今天晚上我們去外面吃飯吧。

B. 好啊。去哪家飯店？

A. 還到那個中國飯店去，怎麼樣？

A. Let's go out for dinner tonight.
  B. Good. Which restaurant?
A. How about going to that Chinese restaurant again?

2.
A. 今天晚上去看電影，怎麼樣？

B. 對不起，今天晚上我有事。

A. How about going to a movie tonight?
  B. Sorry. I'm busy tonight.

3.
A. 謝謝你的光臨。

B. 謝謝你，

我很高興參加這招待會。

A. Thank you for coming.
  B. Thank you.
    I'm delighted to be able to attend this reception.

饭店 fàndiàn
      Restaurant.

电影 diànyǐng
      Movie.

J. MINI DIALOGS: SIMPLIFIED CHARACTERS AND PINYIN

1.
A. 今天晚上我们去外面吃饭吧.

B. 好啊。去哪家饭店？

A. 还到那个中国饭店去，怎么样？

A. Jīntiān wǎnshàng wǒmen qù wàimian chī fàn ba.
B. Hǎo a. Qù něi jiā fàndiàn?
A. Hái dào nèige Zhōngguo fàndiàn qù, zěmme yàng?

2.
A. 今天晚上去看电影，怎么样？

B. 对不起，今天晚上我有事。

A. Jīntiān wǎnshàng qù kàn diànyǐng, zěmme yàng?
B. Duìbuqǐ, jīntiān wǎnshàng wǒ yǒu shì.

3
A. 谢谢你的光临.

B. 谢谢你，
我很高兴参加这招待会。

A. Xièxie nǐde guānglín.
B. Xièxie nǐ.
Wǒ hěn gāoxìng cānjiā zhèi zhāodài huì.

光临 guānglín
Visit of an esteemed guest.

招待会 zhāodài huì
A reception.

Ⅰ (2)

4.
A. 請出示請帖 。

B. 這是我的請帖 。

A. Please show your invitation.
B. Here it is.

5.
A. 這星期五晚上我們有一個 "中文晚會"，
你來參加嗎 ?

B. 太好了 , 我一定參加 。

A. This Friday evening we're having a Chinese party.
Can you come?
B. Great. I'll be sure to come.

6.
A. 你收到新年晚會的請帖了嗎 ?

B. 收到了 。
在人民大會堂舉行 , 是嗎 ?

A. Did you receive an invitation to the New Year's party?
B. Yes I did.
It's at the People's Assembly Hall, isn't it?

出示	chūshì To show.	请帖	qǐngtiē An invitation.
人民	rénmín The people.	会堂	huìtáng Assembly hall.

J (2)

4.
A. 请出示请帖。
B. 这是我的请帖。

A. Qǐng chūshì qǐngtiē.
B. Zhèi shì wǒde qǐngtiē.

5.
A. 这星期五晚上我们有一个"中文晚会"，
你来参加吗？
B. 太好了，我一定参加。

A. Zhèi xīngqī wǔ wǎnshàng wǒmen yǒu yige 'Zhōngwén wǎnhuì'.
Nǐ lái cānjiā ma?
B. Tài hǎole. Wǒ yídìng cānjiā.

6.
A. 你收到新年晚会的请帖了吗？
B. 收到了。
在人民大会堂举行，是吗？

A. Nǐ shōudào xīnnián wǎnhuì de qǐngtiē le ma?
B. Shōudàole.
Zài rénmín dàhuìtáng jǔxíng, shì ma?

晚会	wǎnhuì An evening party.	收到	shōudào To receive.
大会堂	dàhuìtáng The Great Assembly Hall.	举行	jǔxíng To hold a party or meeting.

K. CULTURAL NOTES

Treats and invitations. The Chinese love to treat. When you visit somebody at their home, they will always bring you something to drink immediately. And if it is anywhere near a meal time when you prepare to leave, they will invariably say chīle fàn zài zǒuba[a] (Eat first, then leave). If you happen to arrive while they are eating, the host will insist that you join them—no matter how little is left. The important thing is the show of warmth and welcome—not what they have to offer.

On special occasions like weddings, birthdays, Chinese New Year's, and other holidays, families like to invite relatives and close friends to get together and eat.

If a group of people are dining out, the person who did the inviting pays. If there is no specific inviter, then the wealthiest or oldest or person of highest status will want to pay. If it isn't clear who qualifies, then two or three of the group might claim the honor and playfully argue over who should pay. When you are part of a group, you rarely pay alone for anything. If a group goes somewhere by bus, for example, one person will pay for the whole group.

a. 吃了饭再走吧。

LESSON 10

AT THE DINNER TABLE

在 餐 桌 上

A. DIALOG: PINYIN TRANSCRIPTION

Àiméi:	Fàn hǎole.[1]	1
	Tāngmǔ, Ānnā, nǐmen xiān qǐng ba.[2]	2
	Wǒ hái yǒu yige cài, zuò hǎole[1] jiù lái.	3
Ānnā:	Āyà! Budeliǎo, zěmme zhème duō de cài a!	4
Wáng:	Méi shémme cài, jiācháng biànfàn.	5
	Dàjiā qǐng ba.[2]	6
	Nǐmen liǎngwèi hē jiǔ ma?	7
Ānnā:	Bù, xièxie.	8
	Wǒmen bu hē jiǔ, yě bu chōu yān.	9
Wáng:	Nā chángchang zhèige yú ba.	10
	Wǒ àirén shāo yú shāo de hǎo.	11
Ānnā:	Mmm··· zhèi yú zhēn hǎo chī.	12
Wáng:	Tāngmǔ, zài lái[3] yidiǎr Běijīng yā ma?	13
Tāngmǔ:	Hǎo, xièxie.	14
Wáng:	Nǐmen liǎngwèi shì chī mǐfàn háishi mántou?	15
Ānnā:	Xièxie, buyàole. Wǒ bǎole.	16

B. Dialog: Simplified Characters

爱梅: 饭好了[1]。 　　　　　　　　　　1
　　　汤姆、安娜，你们先请吧[2]。 　　2
　　　我还有一个菜，做好了[1]就来。 　3

安娜: 啊呀！不得了，怎么这么多的菜啊！ 　4

王: 没什么菜，家常便饭， 　　　　　5
　　大家请吧[2]。 　　　　　　　　6
　　你们两位喝酒吗？ 　　　　　　7

安娜: 不，谢谢。 　　　　　　　　8
　　　我们不喝酒，也不抽烟。 　　9

王: 那尝尝这个鱼吧。 　　　　　10
　　我爱人烧鱼烧得好。 　　　　11

安娜: 呣…这鱼真好吃。 　　　　　12

王: 汤姆，再来[3]一点儿北京鸭吗？ 　13

汤姆: 好，谢谢。 　　　　　　　14

王: 你们两位是吃米饭还是馒头。 　　15

安娜: 谢谢，不要了，我饱了。 　　16

C. Dialog: Yale Transcription

Àiméi:	Fàn hǎule.[1]	1
	Tāngmǔ, Ānnā, nǐmen syān chǐng ba.[2]	2
	Wǒ hái yǒu yige tsài, dzwò hǎule[1] jyòu lái.	3
Ānnā:	Āyà! Budelyǎu, dzěmme jème dwō de tsài a!	4
Wáng:	Méi shémme tsài, jyāchǎng byànfàn.	5
	Dàjyā chǐng ba.[2]	6
	Nǐmen lyǎngwèi hē jyǒu ma?	7
Ānnā:	Bù, syèsye.	8
	Wǒmen bu hē jyǒu, yě bu chōu yān.	9
Wáng:	Nā chángchang jèige yú ba.	10
	Wǒ àirén shāu yú shāu de hǎu.	11
Ānnā:	Mmm··· jèi yú jēn hǎu chř.	12
Wáng:	Tāngmǔ, dzài lái[3] yidyǎr Běijīng yā ma?	13
Tāngmǔ:	Hǎu, syèsye.	14
Wáng:	Nǐmen lyǎngwèi shř chř mǐfàn háishr mántou?	15
Ānnā:	Syèsye, buyàule. Wǒ bǎule.	16

D. Dialog: Full Characters

愛梅: 飯好了[1]。 1

湯姆、安娜，你們先請吧[2]。 2

我還有一個菜，做好了[1]就來。 3

安娜: 啊呀！不得了，怎麼這麼多的菜啊！ 4

王: 沒甚麼菜，家常便飯。 5

大家請吧[2]。 6

你們兩位喝酒嗎？ 7

安娜: 不，謝謝。 8

我們不喝酒，也不抽烟。 9

王: 那嘗嘗這個魚吧。 10

我愛人燒魚燒得好。 11

安娜: 嗯…這魚真好吃。 12

王: 湯姆，再來[3]一點兒北京鴨嗎？ 13

湯姆: 好，謝謝。 14

王: 你們兩位是吃米飯還是饅頭？ 15

安娜: 謝謝，不要了，我飽了。 16

E. Dialog: Vocabulary and Notes

餐　cān
To eat; a meal.

酒　jiǔ
Alcoholic drink.

桌　zhuō
A table.

尝　cháng
To taste.

餐桌　cānzhuō
Dinner table.

鱼　yú
Fish.

菜　cài
Green vegetables; a dish or course of a meal.

烧　shāo
To cook.

好吃　hǎo chī
Good tasting, delicious.

不得了　bùdeliǎo
Exclamation expressing an extreme (good or bad): terrific, terrible.

鸭　yā
Duck.

米　mǐ
Uncooked rice.

家常　jiācháng
Commonplace, ordinary home affair.

米饭　mǐfàn
Cooked rice.

便饭　biàn fàn
An informal meal.

馒头　mán·tóu
Steamed bread.

家常便饭　jiācháng biàn fàn
Ordinary meal, nothing special.

饱　bǎo
Eat to the full.

1. <u>hǎole</u>.[a] This shows completion: 'it's ready', 'I'm finished'.

2. <u>qǐng ba</u>.[b] 'Go ahead', 'please (eat)', 'I invite you to (eat)'.

3. <u>lái</u>.[c] (This note appears on page 156.)

　a. 好了　　　　b. 请吧　　　　c. 来

F. Dialog: English

Aimei: The food is ready.   1

         Tom, Anna, you go ahead.   2

         I've got one more dish. I'll come when I finish it.   3

Anna: My gosh! How come there are so many dishes?   4

Wang: It's nothing. Just common everyday food.   5

         Everybody please go ahead.   6

         Do you drink?   7

Anna: No we don't. Thanks, anyway.   8

         We don't drink or smoke.   9

Wang: Taste this fish, then.   10

         My wife is extra good at fixing fish.   11

Anna: Mmm··· this fish is delicious.   12

Wang: Have some more Peking duck, Tom.   13

Tom: Thanks, I will.   14

Wang: Will you have rice, or steamed bread?   15

Anna: Neither, thanks. I'm full.   16

G. SUBSTITUTIONS: FULL CHARACTERS AND ENGLISH

1. 這魚真好吃.   點心
   豆腐   北京鴨
   牛肉   螃蟹

   This <u>fish</u> is really delicious.   snacks
       bean curd   Peking duck
       beef   crab

2. 再來一點兒北京鴨嗎?   麵條
               蝦   水餃
               饅頭   春卷

   Will you have some more <u>Peking duck</u>?   noodles
                           shrimps   meat dumplings
                           steamed bread   spring rolls

3. 你們兩位喝酒嗎?
          抽烟
          喝茶

   Do the two of you <u>drink</u>?
                     smoke
                     drink tea

H. SUBSTITUTIONS: SIMPLIFIED CHARACTERS AND PINYIN

---

1. 这鱼真好吃。   点心

    豆腐   北京鸭

    牛肉   螃蟹

Zhèi yú zhēn hǎo chī.   diǎnxīn
    dòu‧fu   Běijīng yā
    niú ròu   pángxiè

---

2. 再来一点儿北京鸭吗？   面条

          虾   水饺

         馒头   春卷

Zài lái yi diǎr Běijīng yā ma?   miàntiáo
      xiā   shuǐjiǎo
      mán‧tóu   chūnjuǎn

---

3. 你们两位喝酒吗？

      抽烟

     喝茶

Nǐmen liǎngwèi hē jiǔ ma?
      chōu yēn
      hē chá

G (2)

4. 嘗嘗這個魚吧。   冰淇淋
　　　　酒　　　　　　　　　　　饅頭

Taste this <u>fish</u>.   ice cream
　　　　wine   steamed bread

5. 不得了！怎麼這麼<u>多的菜</u>啊？
　　　　　　　　　多的錢
　　　　　　　　　　難
　　　　　　　　　　貴

My gosh! How come <u>there are so many dishes?</u>
　　　　　　　　　you've got so much money
　　　　　　　　　it's so difficult
　　　　　　　　　it's so expensive

6. 我愛人<u>燒魚燒</u>得好。
　　　　寫字寫
　　　　做衣服做
　　　　打字打

My wife is good at <u>cooking fish</u>.
　　　　　　　　　writing characters
　　　　　　　　　making clothes
　　　　　　　　　typing

H (2)

4. 尝尝这个<u>鱼</u>吧。　　　冰淇淋
　　　　酒　　　　　　　　馒头

Chángchang zhèige <u>yú</u> ba.　　bīngqílín
　　　　　　　jiǔ　　　　　　mán·tóu

5. 不得了！怎么这么<u>多的菜</u>啊？
　　　　　　多的钱
　　　　　　难
　　　　　　贵

Bùdeliǎo!　Zěmme zhème <u>duō de cài</u> a?
　　　　　　　　duō de qián
　　　　　　　　nán
　　　　　　　　guì

6. 我爱人<u>烧鱼烧</u>得好。
　　　写字写
　　　做衣服做
　　　打字打

Wǒ àirén <u>shāo yú shāo</u> de hǎo.
　　　　xiě zì xiě
　　　　zuò yī·fú zuò
　　　　dǎ zì dǎ

I. MINI DIALOGS: FULL CHARACTERS AND ENGLISH

1.
A. 你的錢忘在桌上了。

B. 没忘，這是小費。

A. 中國没有小費的呀！

B. 哦，對不起。

A. You forgot your money. It's on the table.
  B. I didn't forget it. That's a tip.
A. We don't tip in China.
  B. Oh, sorry.

2.
A. 吃完了嗎？走吧。

B. 好，我去付錢。

A. 我來付。

B. 這次我來付。

A. 這樣吧，各付各的吧。

A. Have you finished eating? Let's go.
  B. O.K. I'll go pay the bill.
A. I'll get it.
  B. No, it's my turn.
A. Let's do this, then.
    We'll each pay our own.

忘   wàng
      To forget.

小費   xiǎofèi
        Tip.

J. Mini Dialogs: Simplified Characters and Pinyin

1.

A. 你的钱忘在桌上了。

   B. 没忘，这是小费。

A. 中国没有小费的呀！

   B. 哦，对不起。

A. Nǐde qián wàng zài zhuōshàng le.
  B. Méi wàng, zhèi shì xiǎofèi.
A. Zhōngguo méi yǒu xiǎofèi de ya.
  B. Ò, duìbuqǐ.

2.

A. 吃完了吗？走吧。

   B. 好，我去付钱。

A. 我来付。

   B. 这次我来付。

A. 这样吧，
   各付各的吧。

A. Chī wánle ma? Zǒu ba.
  B. Hǎo, wǒ qù fù qián.
A. Wǒ lái fù.
  B. Zhèi cì wǒ lái fù.
A. Zhèi yàng ba.
   Gè fù gè de ba.

付钱　　fù qián
　　　　To pay money.

I (2)

3.
A. 這兒是菜單。
   你喜歡吃甚麼？
   請點菜吧。
   B. 我甚麼都喜歡。

A. Here's the menu.
   What do you like?
   Please order.
   B. I like everything.

4.
A. 我點北京烤鴨。
   你喜歡嗎？
   B. 我嫌這菜太膩．
      我喜歡海味兒．
A. 你不是說甚麼都喜歡嗎？
   B. 哈哈哈...

A. I'll have the roast Peking duck.
   Do you like it?
   B. No, I don't like it. It's too greasy.
      I prefer seafood.
A. Didn't you say you like everything?
   B. Haha.

菜单	càidān Menu	点	diǎn To order.
膩	nì Greasy.	味	wèi Flavor.

J (2)

3.
A. 这儿是菜单。
你喜欢吃什么?
请点菜吧。
B. 我什么都喜欢。

A. Zhèr shì càidān.
Nǐ xǐhuān chī shémme?
Qǐng diǎn cài ba.
B. Wǒ shémme dōu xǐhuān.

4.
A. 我点北京烤鸭。
你喜欢吗?
B. 我嫌这菜太腻。
我喜欢海味儿。
A. 你不是说什么都喜欢吗?
B. 哈哈哈…

A. Wǒ diǎn Běijīng kǎo yā.
Nǐ xǐhuān ma?
B. Wǒ xián zhèi cài, tài nì.
Wǒ xǐhuān hǎiwèr.
A. Nǐ bushì shuō shémme dōu xǐhuān ma?
B. Ha ha ha.

烤　kǎo　To roast or bake.

嫌　xián　To dislike.

海味儿　hǎi wèr　Seafood.

K. CULTURAL NOTES

Chinese eating habits. The times of eating meals in China are quite uniform: breakfast at about seven, lunch at noon, and dinner at six or seven. As in many other parts of the world, the noon meal is the biggest meal on the farms, and the evening meal is the biggest meal in the cities (where lunch is eaten away from home). Meals are usually a bit noisy—both with chatter and with the sounds of eating (open-mouth eating, noisy sipping to cool off hot tea or soup, belching, etc.). Some Westerners may find some of these sounds offensive; but they should not make the mistake of feeling that the Chinese are being impolite—nor that their customs are uncivilized. Think of a culture that requires the suppression of laughter at a good comedy, and you might begin to wonder whether it's your own culture that is strange (or at least arbitrary) in suppressing the natural sounds of enjoying good food.

Having guests for dinner. The host invites you to be seated at the table (qǐng zuò[a]) and to start eating (qǐng chī,[b] or chībạ, chībạ[c]). He will probably stand up, lean over, and put something on your plate. He may keep giving you more of what he thinks you like best. So if you are the type that saves the best for last, you may frequently get into trouble. The host may keep giving you more of what you took first.

E. DIALOG: VOCABULARY AND NOTES (continued from page 146)

3. **lái.**[d] This is neither the main verb (to come) nor the directional auxiliary (see p. 162, note 4). It is a 'pro-verb' (compare '*pro*noun'); that is, it takes the place of a verb just as a pronoun takes the place of a noun. Notice the similar use of the English 'get' in the sentence 'I'll get it.' This can refer to 'answer the telephone', 'open the door', or almost any action verb that is indicated by the situation. The Chinese for these situations is simply **wǒ lái.**[e]

a. 请坐   c. 吃吧，吃吧   e. 我来

b. 请吃   d. 来

LESSON 11

GIVING AND RESPONDING TO COMPLIMENTS

赞 扬 和 谦 虚

A. Dialog: Pinyin Transcription

Ānnā: Àiméi, nǐmen zhēn kèqi,   1

         gěi wǒmen shāole zhème hǎo chīde cài.   2

Àiméi: Hǎo shémme ya![1]   3

         Nǐ chī bǎole ma?   4

Ānnā: Bǎole. Chī dàole hóulong kǒu.   5

         Xiàge xīngqī wǒ dōu[2] kěyǐ bu chī fàn le.   6

Àiméi: Nǐ zhēn ài kāi wánxiào.   7

         Méi shémme chīde.   8

Ānnā: Āiyò, shíge cài yīge tāng,   9

         hái shuō méi shémme chīde?   10

         Nǐ tài kèqi le.   11

         Duìle,   12

         zhèi yi shǒu[3] hǎo cài nǐ cóng nǎr xué láide ya?[4]   13

Àiméi: Āyò, wǒ shì zìjǐ xiā xuéde.   14

         Yàoshi nǐ zhēn xǐhuān wǒde cài,   15

         xiàcì zài qǐng nǐ,   16

         zěmme yàng?   17

Ānnā: Nà tài hǎole.   18

B. DIALOG: SIMPLIFIED CHARACTERS

安娜: 爱梅，你们真客气，   1
    给我们烧了这么好吃的菜。   2

爱梅: 好什么呀[1]!   3
    你吃饱了吗？   4

安娜: 饱了。吃到了喉咙口。   5
    下个星期我都[2]可以不吃饭了。   6

爱梅: 你真爱开玩笑。   7
    没什么吃的。   8

安娜: 哎呀，十个菜一个汤，   9
    还说没什么吃的？   10
    你太客气了。   11
    对了，   12
    这一手[3]好菜你从那儿学来的呀[4]?   13

爱梅: 啊哟，我是自己瞎学的。   14
    要是你真喜欢我的菜，   15
    下次再请你，   16
    怎么样？   17

安娜: 那太好了。   18

C. Dialog: Yale Transcription

Ānnā: Àiméi, nǐmen jēn kèchi,   1

       gěi wǒmen shāule jème hǎu chřde tsài.   2

Àiméi: Hǎu shémme ya![1]   3

       Nǐ chř bǎule ma?   4

Ānnā: Bǎule. Chř dàule hóulung kǒu.   5

       Syàge syīngchī wǒ dōu[2] kěyǐ bu chř fàn le.   6

Àiméi: Nǐ jēn ài kāi wánsyàu.   7

       Méi shémme chřde.   8

Ānnā: Āiyò, shŕge tsài yīge tāng,   9

       hái shwō méi shémme chřde?   10

       Nǐ tài kèchi le.   11

       Dwèile,   12

       jèi yi shǒu[3] hǎu tsài nǐ tsúng nǎr sywé láide ya?[4]   13

Àiméi: Āyò, wǒ shŕ dzìjǐ syā sywéde.   14

       Yàushr nǐ jēn syǐhwān wǒde tsài,   15

       syàtsz̀ dzài chǐng nǐ,   16

       dzěmme yàng?   17

Ānnā: Nà tài hǎule.   18

D. DIALOG: FULL CHARACTERS

安娜：愛梅，你們真客氣，　　　　　　　1
　　　給我們燒了這麼好吃的菜。　　　　2

愛梅：好甚麼呀[1]！　　　　　　　　　　3
　　　你吃飽了嗎？　　　　　　　　　　4

安娜：飽了。吃到了喉嚨口。　　　　　　5
　　　下個星期我都[2]可以不吃飯了。　　6

愛梅：你真愛開玩笑。　　　　　　　　　7
　　　沒甚麼吃的。　　　　　　　　　　8

安娜：哎喲，十個菜一個湯，　　　　　　9
　　　還說沒甚麼吃的？　　　　　　　　10
　　　你太客氣了。　　　　　　　　　　11
　　　對了，　　　　　　　　　　　　　12
　　　這一手[3]好菜你從哪兒學來的呀[4]？　13

愛梅：啊喲，我是自己瞎學的。　　　　　14
　　　要是你真喜歡我的菜，　　　　　　15
　　　下次再請你，　　　　　　　　　　16
　　　怎麼樣？　　　　　　　　　　　　17

安娜：那太好了。　　　　　　　　　　　18

E. DIALOG: VOCABULARY AND NOTES

赞扬   zànyáng
Compliments, to
praise.

谦虚   qiānxū
To be modest.

客气   kè·qi
Polite, gracious,
civil, modest.

喉咙口   hóulong kǒu
The entrance to
the throat.

笑   xiào
To laugh, smile.

汤   tāng
Soup.

自己   zìjǐ
Oneself.

瞎学   xiā xué
To study blindly
(that is, to pick up
some skill without
really trying).

下次   xià cì
Next time,
another time.

1. hǎo shémme.[a] This is just a way of responding to the compliment by denying it: 'What do you mean, good?'

2. dōu.[b] This refers to the 'whole' week, even though it is
grammatically out of place.

3. zhèi yi shǒu hǎo cài.[c] The word shǒu[d] is acting like a
classifier of skill in cooking: this 'hand' (that is, 'kind')
of good cooking.

4. xué láide.[e] The word lái[f] is used here as a 'directional
auxiliary'. It shows the direction of the main verb 'learn'
(*from* a source *to* the learner). It thus focuses on the *re-
ceiving* of the learning.

a. 好什么   c. 这一手好菜   e. 学来的

b. 都   d. 手   f. 来

F. Dialog: English

Anna: It was really gracious of you, Aimei,   1

        to prepare such delicious food for us.   2

Aimei: Oh, it was nothing.   3

        Did you get enough to eat?   4

Anna: I'll say. I'm full to the top of my throat.   5

        I won't have to eat all next week.   6

Aimei: You're quite a joker.   7

        We hardly had anything.   8

Anna: My gosh! Ten courses and a soup,   9

        and you still say there was hardly anything?   10

        You're too modest.   11

        By the way,   12

        where did you learn to cook so well?   13

Aimei: Oh, I just picked it up by myself.   14

        If you really like my cooking so much,   15

        you'll have to come again sometime.   16

        How about it?   17

Anna: That would be great.   18

G. SUBSTITUTIONS: FULL CHARACTERS AND ENGLISH

1.   A. 你燒的菜很好吃。   B. <u>不好不好。</u>

                               好甚麼呀？

                               没甚麼好吃的。

                               是嗎？

                               真的嗎？

    A. Your food's delicious.   B. <u>No it isn't.</u>
                                      How could it be good?
                                      It's not so good.
                                      Is that so?
                                      Really.

---

2.   <u>吃</u> 到了 <u>喉嚨口</u>。

    壞   底

    好   頂

    學   家

<u>I ate</u>	<u>up to the top of my throat.</u>
it was bad	down to the very bottom
it was good	up to the very top
he learned	to perfection

H. Substitutions: Simplified Characters and Pinyin

1.
A. 你烧的菜很好吃。
B. <u>不好不好</u>。
好什么呀？
没什么好吃的。
是吗？
真的吗？

A. Nǐ shāode cài hěn hǎo chī.
B. <u>Bu hǎo, bu hǎo.</u>
Hǎo shémme ya?
Méi shémme hǎo chīde.
Shì ma?
Zhēnde ma?

2.
<u>吃到了喉咙口</u>。
坏　　底
好　　顶
学　　家

<u>Chī</u> dàole <u>hóulong kǒu</u>.
huài　　dǐ
hǎo　　dǐng
xué　　jiā

G (2)

3. 這一手好菜，你從哪裏學來的？
　　一口流利的中國話
　　一手漂亮的書法

　　Where did you learn to cook such good food?
　　　　　　　　　　　　to speak such fluent Chinese
　　　　　　　　　　　　such beautiful handwriting

4. 給我們燒了那麼好　　　的菜。
　　　　做　　　漂亮　　衣服
　　　　講　　　有意思　故事

　　You cooked us such delicious　　food.
　　　　made　　　　beautiful　　clothes
　　　　told　　　　an interesting story

5. 我是自己瞎學的。
　　　　　　做
　　　　　　想
　　　　　　寫

　　I learned it blindly by myself (with no clear method).
　　　did it
　　　thought about it
　　　wrote it

H (2)

3. <u>这 一 手 好菜</u> ，   你 从 哪里 学 来 的 ？
　　一 口 流利 的 中国话
　　一 手 漂亮 的 书法

Zhèi <u>yi shǒu hǎo cài</u>,   nǐ cóng nǎlǐ xué lái de?
yi kǒu liúlì de Zhōngguo huà
yi shǒu piào∘liàng de shūfǎ.

4. 给我们<u>烧</u>了那么<u>好</u>　　的<u>菜</u>。
　　　做　　　漂亮　　衣服
　　　讲　　有意思　　故事

Gěi wǒmen <u>shāo</u> le nàme <u>hǎo</u>   de <u>cài</u>.
　　　zuò　　　　piàoliang　yī∘fú
　　　jiǎng　　　yǒu yìsi　　gù∘shì

5. 我 是 自己 瞎<u>学</u> 的 。
　　　　　做
　　　　　想
　　　　　写

Wǒ shì zìjǐ xiā <u>xué</u> de.
　　　　zuò
　　　　xiǎng
　　　　xiě

I. Mini Dialogs: Full Characters and English

---

1. A. 你的中國話講得真好 。

   B. 不太好 。馬馬虎虎 。

   A. Your Chinese is really good.
   B. It's not very good. Just so so.

---

2. A. 你的中國字寫得真漂亮 。

   B. 哪裏哪裏 ,
      沒有你的漂亮 。

   A. Your Chinese characters are beautiful.
   B. Oh they're not so good.
      Not nearly as beautiful as yours.

---

3. A. 今天你穿得特別漂亮 ,
      我都不認識你了 。

   B. 是嗎 ?

   A. You're dressed extra nice today.
      I couldn't even recognize you.
   B. Really?

哪里   nǎlǐ
        Where? Used to deny a compliment.

J. MINI DIALOGS: SIMPLIFIED CHARACTERS AND PINYIN

1.
> A. 你的中国话讲得真好。
>
> B. 不太好。马马虎虎。

> A. Nǐde Zhōngguo huà jiǎng de zhēn hǎo.
> B. Bu tài hǎo. Máma huhū.

2.
> A. 你的中国字写得真漂亮。
>
> B. 哪里哪里，
>   没有你的漂亮。

> A. Nǐde Zhōngguo zì xiě de zhēn piàoliang.
> B. Nǎlǐ nǎlǐ,
>   méi yǒu nǐde piàoliang.

3.
> A. 今天你穿得特别漂亮，
>   我都不认识你了。
>
> B. 是吗？

> A. Jīntiān nǐ chuān de tèbié piàoliang.
>   Wǒ dōu bu rènshi nǐ le.
> B. Shì ma?

穿   chuān
To put on, to wear.

I (2)

4.

A. 這個學期你的中文進步得很快。

B. 啊，那是因為您老師教得好。

A. Your Chinese has really improved fast this term.
B. Oh, that's because you taught me so well, teacher.

5.

A. 我看見你的女朋友啦！

美極了。

B. 別開玩笑了。

A. I saw your girl friend!
She's really pretty.
B. You're kidding.

6.

A. 你這件衣服真好看。

B. 真的嗎？

A. 真的。你看上去年輕了。

A. Your blouse is really nice looking.
B. Do you really think so?
A. Yes. It makes you look young.

学期   xuéqī
A school term.

老師   lǎoshī
Teacher.

这件衣服   zhèjian yīfu   'This article of clothing.' A is
pointing to B's blouse, hence the English translation.

J (2)

4.
A. 这个学期你的中文进步得很快。
B. 啊，那是因为您老师教得好。

A. Zhèige xuéqī nǐde Zhōngwén jìnbù de hěn kuài.
B. À, nà shì yīnwei nín lǎoshī jiāo de hǎo.

5.
A. 我看见你的女朋友啦！
美极了。
B. 别开玩笑了。

A. Wǒ kànjian nǐde nǚ péngyou la!
Měi jíle.
B. Bié kāi wánxiào le.

6.
A. 你这件衣服真好看。
B. 真的吗？
A. 真的，你看上去年轻了。

A. Nǐ zhèijian yīfu zhēn hǎokàn.
B. Zhēnde ma?
A. Zhēnde. Nǐ kàn shangqu nián qīngle.

啦　la
Similar to le.

看上去　kàn shangqu
To look (young).

年轻　nián qīng
Young.

K. CULTURAL NOTES

Compliments are used similarly in English and Chinese. But responses to compliments differ.

The commonest response to a compliment in English is a thank you. This is completely inappropriate in Chinese. If you thank a Chinese who has just paid you a compliment, he will probably think you have misunderstood.

The two commonest responses to compliments in Chinese are 1) to deny the compliment and 2) to question it.

1. 不好。
   Bu hǎo.
   No, it isn't good.

2. 是吗？
   Shì ma?
   Is that so?

   真的吗？
   Zhēnde ma?
   Really?

Other responses include 3) returning the compliment, 4) saying the complimenter doesn't mean it, and 5) making some sound of denial and changing the subject.

3. 嗳，没有你的好。
   Âi,* méi yǒu nǐde hǎo.
   Oh, it's not as good as yours.

4. 别开玩笑了。
   Bié kāi wánxiào le.
   Don't make a joke. (You're kidding.)

---

*   Interjections have intonations—not tones. They are usually written with the closest tone marker or with no marker at all. Here, the marker ˆ is used for a rising-falling intonation, which is then followed by another rise (ˊ).

LESSON 12

CHINESE CURRENCY

中 国 货 币

A. Dialog: Pinyin Transcription

Ānnā: Wáng jiàoshòu, wǒ xiǎng qǐng jiāo yige wèntí.[1]   1

Wáng: Shémme wèntí ya?   2

Ānnā: Wǒ zhīdào Zhōngguo de huòbì jiàozuò rénmínbì.   3

       Rénmínbì de dānwèi shì yuán, jiǎo, fēn.   4

       Yī yuán děngyu shí jiǎo,   5

       yī jiǎo děngyu shí fēn.   6

       Kěshì zài zhèr wǒ cháng tīng rén shuō   7

       jǐ kuài jǐ máo de.   8

       Zhèi shì wèishémme?   9

Wáng: Ò, zài kǒuyǔ zhōng, yǒu shí,[2] yuán jiàozuo kuài,   10

       jiǎo jiàozuò máo.   11

       Zuì hòu yige fēn zì chángchang shěngqule.   12

Ānnā: Ò.   13

Wáng: Bǐru shuō ba,   14

       bǎ yī yuán sān jiǎo wǔ fēn   15

       shuō chéng[3] yikuài sānmáo wǔ.   16

Ānnā: Ò, wǒ dǒngle. Xièxie.   17

B. DIALOG: SIMPLIFIED CHARACTERS

安娜: 王教授，我想请教一个问题[1]。   1

王: 什么问题呀？   2

安娜: 我知道中国的货币叫做人民币。   3
人民币的单位是圆、角、分。   4
一圆等于十角，   5
一角等于十分。   6
可是在这儿我常听人说   7
几块几毛的，   8
这是为什么？   9

王: 哦，在口语中，有时[2]，圆叫做块，   10
角叫做毛。   11
最后一个分字常常省去了。   12

安娜: 哦！   13

王: 比如说吧，   14
把一圆三角五分   15
说成[3]一块三毛五。   16

安娜: 哦，我懂了，谢谢。   17

C. Dialog: Yale Transcription

Ānnā: Wáng jyàushòu, wǒ syǎng chǐng jyāu yige wèntí.[1]   1

Wáng: Shémme wèntí ya?   2

Ānnā: Wǒ jr̄dàu Jūnggwo de hwòbì jyàudzwò rénmínbì.   3

       Rénmínbì de dānwèi shr̀ ywán, jyāu, fēn.   4

       Yī ywán děngyu shŕ jyǎu,   5

       yī jyǎu děngyu shŕ fēn.   6

       Kěshr̀ dzài jèr wǒ cháng tīng rén shwō   7

       jǐ kwài jǐ máu de.   8

       Jèi shr̀ wèishémme?   9

Wáng: Ò, dzài kǒuyǔ jūng, yǒu shŕ,[2] ywán jyàudzwo kwài,   10

       jyǎu jyàudzwò máu.   11

       Dzwèi hòu yige fēn dž chángchang shěngchyule.   12

Ānnā: Ò.   13

Wáng: Bǐrú shwō ba,   14

       bǎ yī ywán sān jyǎu wǔ fēn   15

       shwō chéng[3] yikwài sānmáu wǔ.   16

Ānnā: Ò, wǒ dǔngle. Syèsye.   17

D. DIALOG: FULL CHARACTERS

安娜：王教授，我想請教一個問題[1]。　　　1

王：　甚麼問題呀？　　　2

安娜：我知道中國的貨幣叫做人民幣。　　　3
　　　人民幣的單位是圓、角、分。　　　4
　　　一圓等於十角，　　　5
　　　一角等於十分。　　　6
　　　可是，在這兒我常聽人說　　　7
　　　幾塊幾毛的，　　　8
　　　這是為甚麼？　　　9

王：　哦，在口語中，有時[2]圓叫做塊，　　　10
　　　角叫做毛。　　　11
　　　最後一個分字常常省去了。　　　12

安娜：哦！　　　13

王：　比如說吧，　　　14
　　　把一圓三角五分　　　15
　　　說成[3]一塊三毛五。　　　16

安娜：哦，我懂了，謝謝。　　　17

E. Dialog: Vocabulary and Notes

货币 huòbì
Coins, currency.

问题 wèntí
A problem.

人民币 rénmínbì
The people's currency.

圆 yuán
Unit of currency, 'dollar'; a circle.

角 jiǎo
A unit of 10 'cents'; a horn, an angle.

分 fēn
One 'cent', one minute; to divide.

等于 děng·yú
To equal.

常 cháng
Often.

块 kuài
Unit of currency, 'dollar'; piece.

毛 máo
Ten 'cents'; hair.

口语 kǒuyǔ
Colloquial speech.

最后 zuì hòu
The last.

省 shěng
To omit, leave out; reduce, save.

比如 bǐrú
For example.

成 chéng
To become.

1. qǐng jiāo yige wèntí.[a] I request you to 'teach' me a problem (that is, 'please explain something to me').

2. yǒu shí = yǒude shíhòu.[b]

3. bǎ x shuō chéng y.[c] To take x and say it as ('becoming') y (that is, 'to say y instead of x).

a. 请教一个问题

c. 把 x 说成 y

b. 有时 = 有的时候

F. Dialog: English

Anna: Professor Wang, I'd like to ask you something.   1

Wang: What is it?   2

Anna: I know Chinese currency is called 'the people's currency',   3

       and that its units are the <u>yuan</u>, <u>jiao</u>, and <u>fen</u>.   4

       And I know one <u>yuan</u> equals ten <u>jiao</u>   5

       and one <u>jiao</u> equals ten <u>fen</u>.   6

       But here I often hear people say   7

       so many <u>kuai</u> and so many <u>mao</u>.   8

       Why is this?   9

Wang: Oh, in colloquial speech, <u>yuan</u> is sometimes called <u>kuai</u>,   10

       and <u>jiao</u> is called <u>mao</u>.   11

       The last word, <u>fen</u>, is often dropped.   12

Anna: Oh.   13

Wang: For example,   14

       1 <u>yuan</u>, 3 <u>mao</u>, 5 <u>fen</u>   15

       is said 1 <u>kuai</u> 3 <u>mao</u> 5.   16

Anna: Oh, I see. Thank you.   17

G. Substitutions: Full Characters and English

1.
人民幣 的 單 位 是 圓 、 角 、 分 。
時間   小時 、 分 、 秒

The units of <u>RMB</u> are <u>dollars, dimes, and pennies</u>.
        <u>time</u>   <u>hours, minutes, and seconds</u>.

2.
在 口 語 中   圓 叫 做   塊 .
日 常 生 活   角   毛
兒 語   母 親   媽媽
            父 親   爸爸

In <u>colloquial speech</u>,   <u>yuán</u> is called <u>kuài</u>.
   daily life   jiǎo   máo
   children's language   mother   mama
                               father   papa

3.
一 圓 等 於 十 角 。
角   十 分
小 時   六 十 分 鐘
年   365 天

One <u>dollar</u> equals <u>10 dimes</u>.
    dime   10 cents
    hour   60 minutes
    year   365 days

H. SUBSTITUTIONS: SIMPLIFIED CHARACTERS AND PINYIN

1.　人民币的单位是圆、角、分。
　　时 间　　　　　小時、分、秒。

　　Rénmínbì de dānwèi shì yuán, jiǎo, fēn.
　　shíjiān　　　　　xiǎoshí, fēn, miǎo

2.　在口语 中 圆 叫做块。
　　日常生活　角　　　毛
　　儿语　　　母亲　　妈妈
　　　　　　父亲　　爸爸

　　Zài kǒuyǔ　　　zhōng yuán jiàozuò kuài.
　　rìchángshēng·huó　　　jiǎo　　　máo
　　ér yǔ　　　　　　　mǔqin　　māma
　　　　　　　　　　　fùqin　　bàba

3.　一圆 等于十角。
　　角　　　十分
　　小时　　六十分钟
　　年　　　365 天

　　Yī yuán　děng·yú shí jiǎo.
　　jiǎo　　　shí fēn
　　xiǎoshí　　liùshí fēnzhōng
　　nián　　　365 tiān

I. Mini Dialogs: Full Characters and English

---

1. A. 這個符號 Rén Mín Bì,
   是甚麼意思 ?

   B. 這是人民幣的拼音,
   縮寫符號是 RMB 。 圓的符號是 ¥ 。

   A. These letters 'Rén Mín Bì',
      what do they mean?
   B. That's the phonetic spelling for <u>rénmínbì</u>.
      The abbreviation is RMB. The symbol for the <u>yuan</u> is ¥.

---

2. A. 中國有紙幣 。
   有沒有硬幣 ?

   B. 有啊 。
   有一分的、二分的、五分的硬幣 ,
   就跟美國的一分硬幣五分硬幣一樣 。

   A. I know China has paper currency,
      but does it also have coins?
   B. Yes.
      We have a 1 <u>fen</u> coin, a 2 <u>fen</u> coin, and a 5 <u>fen</u> coin.
      Just like the American 1 cent and 5 cent coins.

符号 fúhào
Symbols, signs, letters.

缩 suō
To shrink, contract.

拼音 pīnyīn
A phonetic alphabet or transcription.

J. MINI DIALOGS: SIMPLIFIED CHARACTERS AND PINYIN

1.
A. 这个符号 Rén Mín Bì,
  是什么意思？
  B. 这是人民币的拼音，
    缩写符号是 RMB. 圆的符号是 ¥.

A. Zhèige fúhào "Rén Mín Bì"
   shì shémme yìsi?
  B. Zhèi shì rénmínbì de pīnyīn.
     Suō xiě fúhào shì RMB. Yuán de fúhào shì ¥.

2.
A. 中国有纸币。
  有没有硬币？
  B. 有啊。
    有一分的、二分的、五分的硬币，
    就跟美国的一分硬币五分硬币一样。

A. Zhōngguo yǒu zhǐbì.
   Yǒu méi you yìngbì.
  B. Yǒu a.
     Yǒu yī fēn de, èr fēn de, wǔ fēn de yìngbì.
     Jiù gēn Měiguo de yīfēn yìngbì wǔfēn yìngbì yi yàng.

缩写   suōxiě
       To abbreviate.

纸币   zhǐbì
       Paper currency.

硬币   yìngbì
       Coins (hard currency).

I (2)

3.
| A. 一共多少錢 ? |
| B. 一共三百四十六塊五毛三 。 |

A. How much money is it altogether?
  B. Altogether, 346 'dollars' and 53 'cents'. (¥346.53)

4.
| A. 我想把美圓換成人民幣。 |
| 外幣兌換處在哪兒 ? |
| B. 這個旅館裏有一個 。 |

A. I'd like to exchange American dollars for Renminbi.
  Where is there a foreign currency exchange shop?
  B. There's one in this hotel.

5.
| A. 對不起 , |
| 甚麼地方兌換旅行支票 ? |
| B. 銀行裏. |

A. Excuse me,
  where can I get a traveler's check cashed?
  B. At a bank.

| 換成 | huàn chéng
To exchange for. | 外币 | wài bì
Foreign currency. |
| 旅馆 | lǚguǎn
Hotel. | 旅行 | lǚxíng
To travel. |

J (2)

3.
A. 一共多少钱？

B. 一共三百四十六块五毛三。

A. Yígòng duōshǎo qián?
B. Yígòng sānbǎi sìshiliù kuài wǔmáo sān.

4.
A. 我想把美元换成人民币。

外币兑换处在哪儿？

B. 这个旅馆里有一个。

A. Wǒ xiǎng bǎ Měi yuán huàn chéng rénmínbì.
Wài bì duìhuàn chù zài nǎr?
B. Zhèige lǚguǎn lǐ yǒu yíge.

5.
A. 对不起，

什么地方兑换旅行支票？

B. 银行里。

A. Duìbuqǐ,
shémme dìfang duìhuàn lǚxíng zhīpiào?
B. Yínháng lǐ.

兑换 duìhuàn
To exchange.

兑换处 duìhuàn chù
A foreign exchange desk or office.

支票 zhīpiào
A check.

银行 yínháng
A bank.

K. CULTURAL NOTES

The Rénmínbì[a] (people's currency), or RMB for short, is the
only legal currency in China, and it cannot be taken out of the
country.

In 1979, special 'foreign exchange certificates' were issued
for the use of foreign travelers in China. The yuan expressed in
foreign exchange certificates is equivalent in value to the RMB
yuan and can be used only within China. The foreign visitor to
China can exchange his foreign currency into foreign exchange
certificates at the Bank of China or at foreign exchange offices
in big hotels, restaurants, or 'Friendship Stores' (department
stores in the big cities that are especially for the use of foreigners). Before the traveler leaves China, he can exchange back
into foreign currency any foreign exchange certificates he has
left.

a. 人民币

LESSON 13

SHOPPING

买 东 西

A. Dialog: Pinyin Transcription

Shòuhuòyuán: Nín mǎi shémme?   1

Ānnā: Wǒ bu mǎi shémme, kànkan.   2

Shòuhuòyuán: Zhèi xiē cíqì, yínqì, xiǎo gǔdǒng   3

               dōu dài yǒu Zhōngguo tèsè.   4

Ānnā: Zhèi huā píng shì gǔdǒng ma?   5

Shòuhuòyuán: Shì de.   6

Ānnā: Shì duōshǎo nián qián de?   7

Shòuhuòyuán: Yì bǎi nián qián de. Zhèi hěn zhíde mǎide.   8

Ānnā: Ràng wǒ xiǎngxiang, en ··· duōshǎo qián?   9

Shòuhuòyuán: Sì bǎi jiǔshiliù kuài.   10

Ānnā: Sì bǎi kuài, mài bumai?   11

Shòuhuòyuán: Āiyà, duìbuqǐ,   12

               Zhōngguo shāngdiàn lǐ méi yǒu tǎojià huánjià de ya. 13

Ānnā: Ò, hǎo ba, hǎo ba.[1] Zhèi shì wǔ bǎi kuài qián. 13

Shòuhuòyuán: Zhǎo gěi nín sì kuài qián. Xièxie.   15

B. Dialog: Simplified Characters

售货员: 您买什么?   1

安娜: 我不买什么,看看。   2

售货员: 这些瓷器、银器、小古董   3
         都带有中国特色。   4

安娜: 这花瓶是古董吗?   5

售货员: 是的。   6

安娜: 是多少年前的?   7

售货员: 一百年前的,这很值得买的。   8

安娜: 让我想想。嗯…多少钱?   9

售货员: 四百九十六块。   10

安娜: 四百块卖不卖?   11

售货员: 啊呀,对不起,   12
         中国商店里没有讨价还价的呀!   13

安娜: 噢,好吧,好吧[1],这是五百块钱。   14

售货员: 找给您四块钱。谢谢。   15

C. Dialog: Yale Transcription

Shòuhwòywán:	Nín mǎi shémme?	1
Ānnā:	Wǒ bu mǎi shémme, kànkan.	2
Shòuhwòywán:	Jèi syē tsźchì, yínchì, syǎu gǔdǔng	3
	dōu dài yǒu Jūnggwo tèsè.	4
Ānnā:	Jèi hwā píng shr̀ gǔdǔng ma?	5
Shòuhwòywán:	Shr̀ de.	6
Ānnā:	Shr̀ dwōshǎu nyán chyán de?	7
Shòuhwòywán:	Yī bǎi nyán chyán de. Jèi hěn jŕde mǎide.	8
Ānnā:	Ràng wǒ syǎngsyang, en ··· dwōshǎu chyán?	9
Shòuhwòywán:	Sź bǎi jyǒushr lyòu kwài.	10
Ānnā:	Sź bǎi kwài, mài bumai?	11
Shòuhwòywán:	Āiyà, dwèibuchǐ,	12
	Jūnggwo shāngdyàn lǐ méi yǒu tǎujyà hwánjyà de ya.	13
Ānnā:	Ò, hǎu ba, hǎu ba.[1] Jèi shr̀ wǔ bǎi kwài chyán.	14
Shòuhwòywán:	Jǎu gěi nín sź kwài chyán. Syèsye.	15

D. DIALOG: FULL CHARACTERS

售貨員： 您買甚麼？ 　　　　　　　　　　　　　　　1

安娜： 我不買甚麼，看看。 　　　　　　　　　　　2

售貨員：這些瓷器、銀器、小古董 　　　　　　　　3
　　　　都帶有中國特色。 　　　　　　　　　　　4

安娜： 這花瓶是古董嗎？ 　　　　　　　　　　　5

售貨員：是的。 　　　　　　　　　　　　　　　　6

安娜： 是多少年前的？ 　　　　　　　　　　　　7

售貨員：一百年前的。這很值得買的。 　　　　　　8

安娜： 讓我想想。嗯…多少錢？ 　　　　　　　　9

售貨員：四百九十六塊。 　　　　　　　　　　　　10

安娜： 四百塊賣不賣？ 　　　　　　　　　　　　11

售貨員：啊呀，對不起， 　　　　　　　　　　　12
　　　　中國商店裏沒有討價還價的呀！ 　　　　　13

安娜： 噢，好吧，好吧[1]，這是五百塊錢。 　　　14

售貨員：找給你四塊錢，謝謝。 　　　　　　　　　15

E. Dialog: Vocabulary and Notes

售
shòu
To sell.

货
huò
Goods, merchandise.

员
yuán
Officer, employee.

售货员
shòuhuò yuán
Salesperson.

器
qì
Ware, instrument.

瓷器
cíqì
Porcelain, china, crockery.

银器
yínqì
Silver ware, goods made of silver.

古董
gǔdǒng
Antiques, curios.

带有
dài yǒu
To have or carry (characteristics).

特色
tèsè
Characteristics, distinctive feature, peculiarity.

花瓶
huā píng
Flower vase.

值得
zhídé
Worth, worthwhile.

让
ràng
To let, allow.

找
zhǎo
To give change.

找给你钱
(I'll) give you change.

商店
shāngdiàn
Store, shop.

价
jià
Price, value.

讨价还价
tǎojià huánjià
To bargain, discuss price ('talk price return price').

1. With the exclamation Ò,[a] Anna shows both that she understands and that she is sorry for her mistake (Oh, sorry!). She is embarrassed and wants to quickly set things right by paying the correct amount. She uses hǎo ba, hǎo ba[b] to get back on the right track (O.K., here, here ···).

a. 噢   b. 好吧，好吧

F. DIALOG: ENGLISH

Clerk: May I help you?   1

Anna: No. I'm just looking.   2

Clerk: This porcelain, silver ware, and the small antiques   3

        all have distinctively Chinese features.   4

Anna: Is this flower vase an antique?   5

Clerk: Yes.   6

Anna: How old is it?   7

Clerk: A hundred years old. It's really a good buy.   8

Anna: Let me think about it. Hmm... how much is it?   9

Clerk: 496 yuan.   10

Anna: Will you sell it for 400?   11

Clerk: Oh, I'm sorry.   12

        There's no bargaining in the stores in China.   13

Anna: Oh. Sorry about that. O.K., here, here. Here's 500. 14

Clerk: Here's four yuan in change. Thank you.   15

G. SUBSTITUTIONS: FULL CHARACTERS AND ENGLISH

1.

我要買<u>小古董</u>。	鞋子
花瓶	襪子
項鏈	褲子
毛巾	襯衫
床單	內衣
肥皂	內褲
牙膏	大衣
牙刷	帽子
水菓	椅子
蔬菜	桌子
肉	床
雞蛋	書桌
米	燈

I want to buy <u>a small antique.</u>	some shoes
a flower vase	some stockings
a necklace	some trousers
some towels	a shirt
some bed sheets	an undershirt
some soap	some shorts
some tooth paste	a coat
a tooth brush	a hat
some fruit	a chair
some vegetables	a table
some meat	a bed
some eggs	a desk
some rice	a lamp

H. Substitutions: Simplified Characters and Pinyin

1.

我要买<u>小古董</u> 。	鞋子
花瓶	袜子
项链	裤子
毛巾	衬衫
床单	内衣
肥皂	内裤
牙膏	大衣
牙刷	帽子
水果	椅子
蔬菜	桌子
肉	床
鸡蛋	书桌
米	灯

Wǒ yào mǎi <u>xiǎo gǔ dǒng</u>.	xiézi
huā píng	wàzi
xiāngliàn	kùzi
máojīn	chènshān
chuángdān	nèiyī
féizào	nèikù
yágāo	dàyī
yáshuā	màozi
shuǐguǒ	yǐzi
sūcài	zhuōzi
ròu	chuáng
jīdàn	shūzhuō
mǐ	dēng

I. MINI DIALOGS: FULL CHARACTERS AND ENGLISH

1.
A. 您買甚麼 ?

　　B. 有鮮艷一些的毛衣嗎 ?

A. 有 .

A. What would you like to buy?
　B. Do you have sweaters a little brighter than these?
A. Yes we do.

2.
A. 這是我昨天買的毛衣 。

　　我想換一件白顏色的 。

　　B. 啊呀 ,

　　　恐怕我們沒有白的 。

A. 那可以退款嗎 ?

　　B. 可以 .

A. This is a sweater that I bought yesterday.
　I'd like to exchange it for a white one.
　B. I'm sorry.
　　I'm afraid we don't have any white ones.
A. Can I get a refund, then?
　B. Certainly.

鮮艷　xiān yàn
Bright, fresh.

(鮮艳)一些　(xiān yàn) yixiē
A little more (bright).

件　jiān
Classifier for clothes.

恐怕　kǒngpà
I'm afraid that, probably.

J. MINI DIALOGS: SIMPLIFIED CHARACTERS AND PINYIN

1.
A. 您买什么？

B. 有鲜艳一些的毛衣吗？

A. 有。

A. Nín mǎi shémme?
B. Yǒu xiān yàn yixiēde máo yī ma?
A. Yǒu.

2.
A. 这是我昨天买的毛衣。

我想换一件白颜色的。

B. 啊呀，

恐怕我们没有白的。

A. 那可以退款吗？

B. 可以。

A. Zhèi shì wǒ zuótiān mǎide máo yī.
Wǒ xiǎng huàn yi jian bái yánes de.
B. Āyà,
kongpà wǒmen méi yǒu báide.
A. Nā kěyi tuǐkuǎn ma?
B. Kěyi.

毛衣	máo yī A sweater	换	huàn To exchange.
颜色	yán·sè Color.	退款	tuǐkuǎn To give a refund.

I (2)

3.
A. 我想去買些東西。
   你去嗎？
   B. 去哪個百貨商店？
A. 我想去友誼商店。
   一塊兒去吧。

A. I'm going shopping for a few things.
   Do you want to come along?
   B. Which department store are you going to?
A. I thought I'd go to the Friendship Store.
   Let's go together.

4.
A. 這件毛衣不合適，
   給我大一點兒的。
   B. 這件怎麼樣？
A. 這件好。多少錢？
   B. 二十二塊。

A. This sweater doesn't fit.
   Give me a slightly larger one.
   B. How's this one?
A. This one's fine. How much is it?
   B. 22 Yuan.

百货   bǎi huò   百货商店   bǎi huò shāngdiàn
        'Hundred goods'.   A department
                                           store.

J (2)

3.
A. 我想去买些东西。
   你去吗？

   B. 去哪个百货商店？

A. 我想去友谊商店。
   一块儿去吧。

A. Wǒ xiǎng qù mǎi xiē dōngxi.
   Nǐ qù ma?
   B. Qù nèige bǎihuò shāngdiàn?
A. Wǒ xiǎng qù yǒu yí shāngdiàn.
   Yí kuàr qù ba.

4.
A. 这件毛衣不合适，
   给我大一点儿的。

   B. 这件怎么样？

A. 这件好。多少钱？

   B. 二十二块。

A. Zhèi jiān máo yī bu héshì,
   gěi wo dà yidiǎr de.
   B. Zhèijiān zěmme yàng?
A. Zhèijiān hǎo. Duōshǎo qián?
   B. Èrshi èr kuài.

友谊 yǒu yí   一块儿 yí kuàr
      Friendship.   Together.

K. CULTURAL NOTES

Bargaining. The procurement and distribution of commodities
in China is mainly done by state organizations. They handle more
than 90 percent of the country's retail sales. In addition to
the state-owned organizations, there are also cooperative stores
and market fairs in the towns and countryside. All government-
run shops have fixed prices. The few cases of non-government-run
shops must operate within strict limits imposed by the government.
These limits are usually about ten to twenty percent above or
below the government-shop prices. So even here, the margin for
bargaining is small.

LESSON 14

GOOD WISHES

祝　愿

A. DIALOG: PINYIN TRANSCRIPTION

Àiméi: Ānnā, zhù nǐ shēngri kuàile.   1

Ānnā: Xièxie nǐ.   2

Àiméi: Zhèi shì wǒmen sòng gěi nǐ de chángshòu miàntiáo.   3

          Zhōngguo rén guò shēngri chī miàntiáo.   4

          Miàntiáo hěn cháng, biǎoshi cháng shòu.   5

Ānnā: Nǐ xiǎng de zhēn zhōudào.   6

Wáng: Tāngmǔ, nǐ gěi Ānnā sòngle shémme shēngri lǐwù a?   7

Tāngmǔ: Wǒde lǐwù shì péi tā lǚxíng bàng e Zhōngguo.   8

          Wǒ yǐ wěituō Zhōngguo lǚxíng shè   9

          ānpái zhèi cì lǚxíng.   10

          Dì yī ge dìdiǎn shì cháng chéng.   11

Zhòng: Yò!   Zhèige lǐwù zhēn bucuò ya!   12

Ānnā: Nǐmen dàjiā qǐng chī diǎr shēngri dàngāo ba.   13

Àiméi: Wǒmen xiān chàngle "zhù nǐ shēngri kuàile" yǐhòu   14

          zài chī, zěmme yàng?   15

Zhòng: Hǎo a!   16

B. DIALOG: SIMPLIFIED CHARACTERS

爱梅: 安娜，祝你生日快乐。 1

安娜: 谢谢你。 2

爱梅: 这是我们送给你的长寿面条。 3
中国人过生日吃面条。 4
面条很长，表示长寿。 5

安娜: 你想得真周到。 6

王: 汤姆，你给安娜送了什么生日礼物啊? 7

汤姆: 我的礼物是陪她旅行半个中国。 8
我已委托中国旅行社 9
安排这次旅行。 10
第一个地点是长城。 11

众: 哟！这个礼物真不错呀！ 12

安娜: 你们大家请吃点儿生日蛋糕吧。 13

爱梅: 我们先唱了"祝你生日快乐"以后 14
再吃,怎么样? 15

众: 好啊！ 16

C. DIALOG: YALE TRANSCRIPTION

| Àiméi: | Ānnā, jù nǐ shēngr kwàile. | 1 |

| Ānnā: | Syèsye nǐ. | 2 |

Àiméi:	Jèi shr̀ wǒmen sùng gěi nǐ de chángshòu myàntyáu.	3
	Jūnggwo rén gwò shēngr chr̄ myàntyáu.	4
	Myàntyáu hěn cháng, byǎushr cháng shòu.	5

| Ānnā: | Nǐ syǎng de jēn jōudàu. | 6 |

| Wáng: | Tāngmǔ, nǐ gěi Ānnā sùngle shémme shēngr lǐwù a? | 7 |

Tāngmǔ:	Wǒde lǐwù shr̀ péi tā lyǔsyíng bànge Jūnggwo.	8
	Wǒ yǐ wěitwō Jūnggwo lyǔsyíng shè	9
	ānpái jèi tsz̀ lyǔsyíng.	10
	Dì yǐ ge dìdyǎn shr̀ cháng chéng.	11

| Jùng: | Yò! Jèige lǐwù jēn butswò ya! | 12 |

| Ānnā: | Nǐmen dàjyā chǐng chr̄ dyǎr shēngr dàngāu ba. | 13 |

| Àiméi: | Wǒmen syān chàngle "jù nǐ shēngr kwàile" yǐhòu | 14 |
| | dzài chr̄, dzěmme yàng? | 15 |

| Jùng: | Hǎu a! | 16 |

D. DIALOG: FULL CHARACTERS

愛梅：安娜，祝你生日快樂。 1

安娜：謝謝你。 2

愛梅：這是我們送給你的長壽麵條。 3
中國人過生日吃麵條。 4
麵條很長，表示長壽。 5

安娜：你想得真周到。 6

王：湯姆，你給安娜送了甚麼生日禮物啊？ 7

湯姆：我的禮物是陪她旅行半個中國。 8
我已委托中國旅行社 9
安排這次旅行。 10
第一個地點是長城。 11

眾：喲！這個禮物真不錯呀！ 12

安娜：你們大家請吃點兒生日蛋糕吧。 13

愛梅：我們先唱了"祝你生日快樂"以後 14
再吃,怎麼樣？ 15

眾：好啊！ 16

E. DIALOG: VOCABULARY AND NOTES

祝愿
zhùyuàn
Good wishes (that is, wishing someone else something, like a happy birthday).

生日
shēng•rì
Birthday.

快乐
kuài•lè
Happiness.

送给
sòng gěi
To present to.

寿
shòu
Long life, longevity.

长寿
cháng shòu
Long life.

面条
miàntiáo
Noodles.

过生日
guò shēngri
To pass (celebrate) one's birthday.

表示
biǎo•shì
To express, stand for.

周到
zhōudào
Thoughtful, considerate.

礼物
lǐwù
Gift, present.

陪
péi
To accompany.

已(经)
yǐ (jīng)
Already.

委托
wěituō
To ask someone to do something; to entrust.

社
shè
Organization, group.

旅行社
lǚxíng shè
Travel service.

安排
ānpái
To arrange.

地点
dìdiǎn
Place, location.

长城
cháng chéng
The Great Wall.

蛋糕
dàngāo
Cake.

唱
chàng
To sing.

F. DIALOG: ENGLISH

| Aimei: | Happy birthday, Anna. | 1 |

Anna: Thank you.   2

Aimei: Here are the 'long-life noodles' that we're giving you. 3
        The Chinese celebrate their birthdays with noodles.   4
        Noodles are very long and thus stand for long life.   5

Anna: How very thoughtful of you.   6

Wang: What are you giving Anna for her birthday, Tom?   7

Tom: My present is to take her on a trip around half of China. 8
        I've already asked the China Travel Service   9
        to arrange the trip.   10
        The first place is the Great Wall.   11

All: Boy! That's some present!   12

Anna: Please have some birthday cake, everybody.   13

Aimei: Let's first sing 'Happy Birthday to You'   14
        and then eat. O.K.?   15

All: O.K.   16

G. SUBSTITUTIONS: FULL CHARACTERS AND ENGLISH

1. 祝你生日快樂.　　　　　　幸福
　　新年愉快　　　　　　　成功
　　聖誕節愉快　　　　　　身體健康

   I wish you a happy birthday.　　happiness
   　　　　　a happy New Year　　　success
   　　　　　a merry Christmas　　　good health

2. 麵條很長表示長壽.
　太陽　亮　　前途光明
　龍　　大　　強大

   Noodles are very long, so they signify long life.
   the sun   bright   a bright future
   a dragon   big   strength

3. 我們先唱歌兒再吃,　　　　　怎麼樣?
　　吃飯　　吃生日蛋糕
　　休息　　踢足球

   How would it be if we sang first and then ate?
   　　　　　　　　　ate the meal   ate the birthday cake
   　　　　　　　　　rested   played football

H. Substitutions: Simplified Characters and Pinyin

1. 祝你<u>生日快乐</u> 。   幸福
        新年愉快   成功
        圣诞节愉快   身体健康

    Zhù nǐ <u>shēng•rì kuài•lè</u>.   xìngfú
            xīn nián yúkuài   chénggōng
            shèngdàn jié yúkuài   shēn•tǐ jiànkāng

2. <u>面条</u> 很<u>长</u> 表示 <u>长寿</u> 。
    太阳   亮   前途光明
    龙   大   强大

    <u>Miàntiáo</u> hěn <u>cháng</u>, biǎo•shì <u>cháng shòu</u>.
    tài•yáng   liàng   qiántú guāngmíng
    lóng   dà   qiángdà

3. 我们先<u>唱歌儿</u> 再<u>吃</u>,   怎么样？
        吃饭   吃生日蛋糕
        休息   踢足球

    Wǒmen xiān <u>chàng gēr</u> zài <u>chī</u>,   zěmme yàng.
              chī fàn   chī shēngri dàn gāo
              xiū•xí   tī zúqiú

I. MINI DIALOGS: FULL CHARACTERS AND ENGLISH

1.
A. 新年好 。	B. 新年好 。
A. Happy New Year.	B. Happy New Year.

2.
A. 春節好 。	B. 春節好 。
A. Happy Chinese New Year.	B. The same to you.

3.
A. 祝你聖誕節愉快 。	B. 聖誕節愉快 。
A. Merry Christmas.	B. Merry Christmas.

4.
A. 湯姆，下星期六晚上
請你和你太太參加我們的婚禮 。
B. 好，一定去 。恭喜恭喜 。

A. Next Saturday evening, Tom,
   I'd like to invite you and your wife to our wedding.
B. Great! I'll be there for sure. Congratulations!

春节	chūn jié Chinese New Year. (Spring Festival.)	圣诞节	shèngdàn jié Christmas.
婚礼	hūnlǐ Wedding ceremony.	恭喜	gōng·xǐ Felicitations.

J. MINI DIALOGS: SIMPLIFIED CHARACTERS AND PINYIN

1.
A. 新年好。
A. Xīnnián hǎo.

B. 新年好。
B. Xīnnián hǎo.

2.
A. 春节好。
A. Chūn jié hǎo.

B. 春节好。
B. Chūn jié hǎo.

3.
A. 祝你圣诞节愉快。
A. Zhù nǐ shèngdàn jié yúkuài.

B. 圣诞节愉快。
B. Shèngdàn jié yúkuài.

4.
A. 汤姆，下星期六晚上
请你和你太太参加我们的婚礼。
B. 好，一定去。恭喜恭喜。

A. Tāngmǔ, xià xīngqī liù wǎnshàng
qǐng nǐ hé nǐ tàitai cānjiā wǒmende hūnlǐ.
B. Hǎo, yídìng qù. Gōngxi gōngxi!

愉快　yúkuài
Happiness.

参加　cānjiā
To take part in,
participate.

I (2)

5.
A. 祝你身體健康。	B. 謝謝。
A. I wish you good health.	B. Thank you.

6.
A. 我提議為我們的友誼和合作
乾杯。
B. 乾杯。

A. I propose a toast to our friendship and cooperation.
   Bottoms up!
B. Bottoms up!

7.
A. 新郎新娘，恭喜恭喜啊。
   B. 祝你們幸福。
      C. 祝你們婚姻美滿。
         D. 謝謝各位。

A. Best wishes to the bride and groom.
   B. I wish you happiness.
      C. I wish you a happy married life.
         D. Thank you, all of you.

健康	jiànkāng Health, healthy.	提议	tí yì To make a toast, proposal, or motion.
新郎	xīn láng The groom.	新娘 xīn niáng The bride.	婚姻 hūnyīn Marriage.

J (2)

5.
A. 祝你身体健康。　　B. 谢谢。

A. Zhù nǐ shēnti jiànkāng.　　B. Xièxie.

6.
A. 我提议为我们的友谊和合作
　　干杯！

B. 干杯！

A. Wǒ tí yì wèi wǒmende yǒu yí hé hézuò
　　Gānbēi.
B. Gānbēi.

7.
A. 新郎新娘，恭喜恭喜啊。

B. 祝你们幸福。

C. 祝你们婚姻美满。

D. 谢谢各位。

A. Xīn láng xīn niáng, gōngxi gōngxi a.
B. Zhù nǐmen xìngfú.
C. Zhù nǐmen hūnyīn měimǎn.
D. Xièxie gè wèi.

合作　hézuò
　　To cooperate.

干杯　gānbēi
　　Bottoms up (dry cup).

美满　měimǎn
　　Full, happy, perfect
　　(especially in marriage).

各位　gè wèi
　　Each person.

K. CULTURAL NOTES

Chinese holidays. There are seven national holidays during which the people (or certain groups of people) get days off.

1. New Year's Day (<u>Xīn nián</u> or <u>Yuán dàn</u>): January 1.
2. Spring Festival or the Lunar New Year or Chinese New Year's (<u>Chūn jié</u>): late January or early February (officially three days off, but a lot more than this in the countryside).
3. Women's Day (<u>Fùnǔ jié</u>): March 8.
4. Workers' Day (<u>Láodòng jié</u>): May 1.
5. Youths' Day (<u>Qīngnián jié</u>): May 4.
6. Children's Day (<u>Értóng jié</u>): June 1.
7. National Day (<u>Guóqìng jié</u>): October 1.

In addition to these national holidays there are several traditional festivals that are very popular.

8. The Lantern Festival (<u>Yuán xiāo jié</u>): 15th day of 1st lunar month. The houses are decorated with lanterns, and the people participate in lion and dragon dances and walk on stilts.

9. Pure Brightness Day (<u>Qīng míng jié</u>): 4th day of 4th lunar month. People go to the graves of their ancestors to pay respect.

10. The Dragon Boat Festival (<u>Duān wǔ jié</u> or <u>Lóng chuán jié</u>): 5th day of 5th lunar month. This festival commemorates a famous poet of about 300 B.C. who drowned himself in protest against the rulers.

11. The Mid-Autumn Festival (<u>Zhōng qiū jié</u>): 15th day of 8th lunar month. This is the brightest full moon of the year (the Western 'Harvest moon'). Moon cakes are eaten.

12. The Double Ninth Festival (<u>Chóng yáng jié</u>): 9th day of 9th lunar month. This festival is concerned with 'climbing high to avoid disaster', and many people go to the mountains.

1. 新年   3.妇女节   6. 儿童节   9. 清明节   11.中秋节

   元旦   4.劳动节   7. 国庆节   10.端午节   12.重阳节

2. 春节   5.青年节   8.元宵节   龙船节

LESSON 15

THE GREAT WALL

长　城

A. Dialog: Pinyin Transcription

Ānnā: Ha hā!* Wǒmen zhōngyú dēng shàngle cháng chéng.   1

Tāngmǔ: Wǒ cháng tīng Zhōngguo rén shuō: 2

           "Bu dào cháng chéng fēi hǎo hàn."[1]   3

Ānnā: Wǒmen dàole cháng chéng le,   4

           wǒmen shì hǎo hàn le.   5

Tāngmǔ: Nǐ kànle zhèige jièshào[2]le méi yǒu?   6

Ānnā: Hái méi ne.   7

Tāngmǔ: Nǐ kàn, nà shàngmian shuō   8

           cháng chéng yǒu liùqiān duō gōng lǐ cháng.   9

Ānnā: Hèi! Zhēn cháng a!   10

Tāngmǔ: Liǎngqiān duō nián qián jiù kāishǐ xiūjiànle.   11

Ānnā: Zhēn liǎobuqǐ.   12

Tāngmǔ: Guàibude hěn duō rén dōu xiǎng   13

           "Dào cǐ yi yóu."   14

           Nǐ kàn, qiáng shang xiěle nàme duō de   15

           "Zhāng Sān[3] dào cǐ yi yóu, Lǐ Sì[3] dào cǐ yi yóu."   16

* See page 172.

B. Dialog: Simplified Characters

安娜: 哈哈！我们终于登上了长城。   1

汤姆: 我常听中国人说：   2
"不到长城非好汉。"[1]   3

安娜: 我们到了长城了，   4
我们是好汉了。   5

汤姆: 你看了这个介绍[2]了没有？   6

安娜: 还没呢。   7

汤姆: 你看，那上面说   8
长城有六千多公里长。   9

安娜: 嘿！真长啊！   10

汤姆: 两千多年前就开始修建了。   11

安娜: 真了不起。   12

汤姆: 怪不得很多人都想   13
"到此一遊"。   14
你看，墙上写了那么多的   15
"张三[3]到此一遊"，"李四[3]到此一遊"。   16

C. Dialog: Yale Transcription

Ānnā: Ha hā![*] Wǒmen jūngyú dēng shàngle cháng chéng.   1

Tāngmǔ: Wǒ cháng tīng Jūnggwo rén shwō: 2

           "Bu dàu cháng chéng fēi hǎu hàn."[1]   3

Ānnā: Wǒmen dàule cháng chéng le,   4

           wǒmen shř hǎu hàn le.   5

Tāngmǔ: Nǐ kànle jèige jyèshàu[2] le méi yǒu?   6

Ānnā: Hái méi ne.   7

Tāngmǔ: Nǐ kàn, nà shàngmyan shwō   8

           cháng chéng yǒu lyòuchyān dwō gūng lǐ cháng.   9

Ānnā: Hèi! Jēn cháng a!   10

Tāngmǔ: Lyǎngchyān dwō nyán chyán jyòu kāishř syōujyànle.   11

Ānnā: Jēn lyǎubuchǐ.   12

Tāngmǔ: Gwàibude hěn dwō rén dōu syǎng   13

           "Dàu tsž yi yóu."   14

           Nǐ kàn, chyáng shang syěle nàme dwō de   15

           "Jāng Sān[3] dàu tsž yi yóu, Lǐ Sž[3] dàu tsž yi yóu."   16

* See page 172.

D. DIALOG: FULL CHARACTERS

安娜：哈哈！我們終於登上了長城。　　　　　　1

湯姆：我常聽中國人說：　　　　　　　　　　　2
　　　"不到長城非好漢"[1]。　　　　　　　　　3

安娜：我們到了長城了，　　　　　　　　　　　4
　　　我們是好漢了。　　　　　　　　　　　　5

湯姆：你看了這個介紹[2]沒有？　　　　　　　　6

安娜：還沒呢。　　　　　　　　　　　　　　　7

湯姆：你看，那上面說　　　　　　　　　　　　8
　　　長城有六千多公里長。　　　　　　　　　9

安娜：嘿！真長啊！　　　　　　　　　　　　　10

湯姆：兩千多年前就開始修建了。　　　　　　　11

安娜：真了不起。　　　　　　　　　　　　　　12

湯姆：怪不得很多人都想　　　　　　　　　　　13
　　　"到此一遊"。　　　　　　　　　　　　　14
　　　你看，墙上寫了那麼多的　　　　　　　　15
　　　"張三[3]到此一遊"，"李四[3]到此一遊"。　16

E. Dialog: Vocabulary and Notes

终于   zhōngyú
Finally, at last,
after all.

登   dēng
To mount, ascend.

非   fēi
Not.

上面   shàng·miàn
On.

多   duō
'More than' the
preceding number.

公里   gōng lǐ
Kilometer.

修建   xiūjiàn
To build.

了不起   liǎobuqǐ
Extraordinary,
unusual.

游   yóu
To travel, tour.

到此一游   dào cǐ yi yóu
To have
traveled to
this place.

墙   qiáng
A wall.

1. hǎo hàn.[a] The word hàn[b] is the name of the Han Dynasty. It
is now used to refer to the Chinese race (as opposed to the
other races living in China). Here, it refers to the quality
of a person, though, instead of the race: a real man (or
woman), a hero (or heroine).

2. jièshào.[c] As in English, this can refer to either the act of
introducing people or to the introduction to a book. Unlike
English, it can also be used to refer to information 'introducing' some place or thing. Here, the information is written
on a board.

3. zhāng sān, lǐ sì.[d] These are fictional names commonly used
for examples, like the English 'Tom, Dick, and Harry'.

4. Literally, 'You're not a real man (or a real person)'.

a. 好汉   b. 汉   c. 介绍   d. 张三，李四

F. DIALOG: ENGLISH

Anna: Ha! We've finally mounted the Great Wall.   1

Tom: I've often heard Chinese people say   2

       "You haven't really lived until you've been to the Great Wall!" 3

Anna: We've been to the Great Wall now   4

       so we've really lived.   5

Tom: Did you see the information here on this board?   6

Anna: No, not yet.   7

Tom: Look. It says here that   8

       the Great Wall is over 6,000 kilometers long.   9

Anna: Boy! That's really something!   10

Tom: They began building it 2,000 years ago.   11

Anna: Really extraordinary!   12

Tom: No wonder so many people think   13

       'I was here.'   14

       Look at what they've all written on the wall.   15

       'Zhang San was here', 'Li Si was here.'   16

G. SUBSTITUTIONS: FULL CHARACTERS AND ENGLISH

1.
長城有多長 ?　　　　海 有多 深 ?
這樓　　高　　　　　月亮　　　遠
這船　　重　　　　　溫度　　　高

How long is the Great Wall?　　How deep is the ocean?
　　high　　　　　building　　　　far　　　　moon
　　heavy　　　　 ship　　　　　　high　　　 temperature

2.
六千多公里 .　　　　　四百多塊錢 .
兩千　年　　　　　　　一百　　個人
五十　歲　　　　　　　十　　　本書

More than 6,000 kilometers.　　More than 400 dollars.
　　　　　 2,000 years　　　　　　　　　100 people
　　　　　　 50 years old　　　　　　　　 10 books

3.
　　公元前兩百年左右 .
大約公元前兩百年
大概公元前兩百年

About 200 years B.C.
About 200 years B.C.
About 200 years B.C.

H. SUBSTITUTIONS: SIMPLIFIED CHARACTERS AND PINYIN

1.
长城有多长？   海　有多深？
这楼　　高   月亮　　远
这船　　重   温度　　高

Cháng chéng yǒu duō cháng?   Hǎi   yǒu duō shēn?
zhèi lóu   gāo   yuè·liàng   yuǎn
zhèi chuán   zhòng   wēndù   gāo

2.
六千　多公里。   四百　多块钱。
两千　　年   一百　　个人
五十　　岁   十　　　本书

Liùqiān   duō gōng lǐ.   Sìbǎi duō kuài qián.
liǎngqiān   nián   yìbǎi   ge rén
wǔshí   suì   shí   běn shū

3
　　公元前两百年左右。
大约公元前两百年
大概公元前两百年

　　Gōngyuán qián liǎng bǎi nián zuǒyòu.
Dàyuè gōngyuán qián liǎng bǎi nián
Dàgài gōngyuán qián liǎng bǎi nián

G (2)

4. 你到過<u>長城</u>　　　嗎？
　　　　故宮
　　　　地下宮殿
　　　　頤和園
　　　　龍門石窟

Have you ever been to the <u>Great Wall</u>?
                          Palace Museum (Forbidden City)
                          Underground Palace
                          Summer Palace
                          Dragon Gate Grotto

5. 我常聽中國人說：
"<u>不到長城非好漢</u>"。
"活到老，學到老"。
"少說話，多做事"。
"失敗是成功之母"。
"眼不見，心不煩"。
"不怕慢，就怕站"。

I have often heard Chinese say:

"<u>You're not a real man until you've been to the Great Wall.</u>"
"If you live to old age, study to old age."
"Talk less, work more."
"Failure is the mother of success."
"What the eye doesn't see, the heart doesn't worry about."
"Don't be afraid to go slowly; just be afraid to stand still."

H (2)

4.　你到过 长城　　　吗？
　　　　　故宫
　　　　　地下宫殿
　　　　　颐和园
　　　　　龙门石窟

　Nǐ dàoguo cháng chéng　ma?
　　　gùgōng
　　　dìxià gōngdiàn
　　　yíhéyuán
　　　lóngmén shíkū

5.　我常听中国人说：
　"不到长城非好汉"。
　"活到老，学到老"。
　"少说话，多做事"。
　"失败是成功之母"。
　"眼不见，心不烦"。
　"不怕慢，就怕站"。

　Wǒ cháng tīng Zhōngguo rén shuō:

　"Bú dào cháng chéng, fēi hǎo hàn."
　"Huó dào lǎo, xué dào lǎo."
　"Shǎo shuō huà, duō zuò shì."
　"Shībài shì chénggōng zhi mǔ."
　"Yǎn bú jiàn, xīn bù fán."
　"Bú pà màn; jiù pà zhàn."

I. Mini Dialogs: Full Characters and English

1.
A. 你到過長城嗎？

B. 到過，你呢？

A. 沒有。很想去看看。

A. Have you ever been to the Great Wall?
  B. Yes. Have you?
A. No, but I'd sure like to go and see it.

2.
A. 長城有多長？

B. 六千多公里。

A. 那麼長啊！

A. How long is the Great Wall?
  B. Over 6,000 kilometers.
A. Boy, what a long wall!

3.
A. 我一定要到長城去看看。

B. 對，你一定要去，
  "不到長城非好漢"。

A. I sure do want to go see the Great Wall.
  B. Yes, you really should.
    "You're not a real man until you've been there."

J. MINI DIALOGS: SIMPLIFIED CHARACTERS AND PINYIN

1.
> A. 你到过长城吗？
>
> B. 到过，你呢？
>
> A. 没有。很想去看看。
>
> A. Nǐ dàoguo cháng chéng ma?
> B. Dàoguo. Nǐ ne?
> A. Méi you. Hěn xiǎng qù kànkan.

2.
> A. 长城有多长？
>
> B. 六千多公里。
>
> A. 那么长啊！
>
> A. Cháng chéng yǒu duō cháng?
> B. Liùqiān duō gōnglǐ.
> A. Nàme cháng a!

3.
> A. 我一定要到长城去看看。
>
> B. 对，你一定要去，
>   "不到长城非好汉。"
>
> A. Wǒ yídìng yào dào cháng chéng qù kànkan.
> B. Duì, nǐ yídìng yào qù.
>   "Búdào cháng chéng fēi hǎo hàn."

I (2)

4.
   A. 聽說，開始時長城没有那麼長。

   B. 對對對。
      公元前兩百年左右，
      一段一段的城墙給連了起來，
      變成現在那麼長的長城了。

   A. I've heard that the Great Wall wasn't so long at first.
   B. That's right.
      About 200 B.C.
      different older walls were joined together
      and became the present Great Wall that is so long.

5.
   A. 游長城該穿甚麼鞋呀？

   B. 千萬別穿高跟鞋。
      長城很高，
      穿了高跟鞋，你上不去，也下不來。

   A. What kind of shoes should you wear to visit the Great Wall?
   B. Well, don't wear high-heeled shoes, by all means.
      The Great Wall is very high.
      And if you wore high-heeled shoes you couldn't get up or down.

…时 = …的时候

公元 gōngyuán
      The Christian era.

城墙 chéng qiáng
      City wall, bulwark.

給 = 被 gěi = bèi
         Passive voice.

鞋 xié
    Shoes.

千万 qiānwàn
      By all means.

J (2)

4.
A. 听说，开始时长城没有那么长。
B. 对对对。
公元前两百年左右，
一段一段的城墙给连了起来，
变成现在那么长的长城了。

A. Tīngshuō kāishǐ shí cháng chéng méi yǒu nàme cháng.
B. Duì duì duì.
Gōngyuán qián liǎngbǎi nián zuǒyòu,
yíduàn yíduànde chéngchiáng gěi liánle qǐ lái,
biàn chéng xiànzài nàme chángde cháng chéng le.

5.
A. 游长城该穿什么鞋呀？
B. 千万别穿高跟鞋。
长城很高，
穿了高跟鞋，你上不去，也下不来。

A. Yóu cháng chéng gāi chuān shémme xié ya?
B. Qiānwàn bié chuān gāo gēn xié.
Cháng chéng hěn gāo.
Chuānle gāo gēn xié, nǐ shàng buqù, yě xià bu lái.

左右	zuǒyòu About.	一段	yī duàn A piece, section.
连	lián To connect.	变成	biàn chéng To change into.
高跟鞋	gāo gēn xié High-heeled shoes.		

K. CULTURAL NOTES

The Great Wall. The Chinese call this the 10,000-li great wall (<u>wàn lǐ cháng chéng</u>). Actually, it is over 12,000 li long (more than 3,750 miles). Over 2,000 years ago, several northern states built walls for protection against the northern barbarians. These separate walls were then joined together during the Chin (Qín) dynasty to protect the newly unified China from northern invasions.

The Chinese Dynasties. A list of the dynasties (or groups of dynasties) is given below.

Hsia	2100-1600 B.C.	夏	Xià
Shang	1600-1100 B.C.	商	Shāng
Western Chou	1100- 771 B.C.	西周	Xī Zhōu
Spring and Autumn Period	770- 476 B.C.	春秋	Chūn Qiū
Warring States Period	475- 221 B.C.	战国	Zhàn Guó
Chin (Ch'in)	221- 207 B.C.	秦	Qín
Han	206 B.C.- 220 A.D.	汉	Hàn
Three Kingdoms	220- 265 A.D.	三国	Sān Guó
Tsin (Chin)	265- 420 A.D.	晋	Jìn
Southern and Northern Ds.	420- 581 A.D.	南北朝	Nán Běi Cháo
Sui	581- 618 A.D.	隋	Suí
Tang (T'ang)	618- 907 A.D.	唐	Táng
Five Dynasties	907- 960 A.D.	五代	Wǔ Dài
Sung	960-1279 A.D.	宋	Sòng
Yuan (Yüan)	1271-1368 A.D.	元	Yuán
Ming	1368-1644 A.D.	明	Míng
Ching (Ch'ing)	1644-1911 A.D.	清	Qīng

LESSON 16

AT THE HOTEL

在 旅 馆

A. Dialog: Pinyin Transcription

Tāngmǔ:	Duìbuqǐ, wǒ shì Tāngmǔ Gélín.	1
Fúwùyuán:	Nín hǎo.	2
Tāngmǔ:	Lǚxíng shè gěi wǒmen dìngle fángjiān le ma?	3
Fúwùyuán:	Dìngle.	4
	Zhèi shì yàoshi. Sì hào fángjiān.	5
Tāngmǔ:	Cāntīng zài nǎlǐ?	6
Fúwùyuán:	Zhōng cāntīng háishi xī cāntīng?	7
Tāngmǔ:	Zhōng cāntīng.	8
Fúwùyuán:	Zài yī lóu.	9
Tāngmǔ:	Chūzū qìchē zěmme jiàode?	10
Fúwùyuán:	Jiào qìchē	11
	gēn fúwù tái shuō yixià jiù xíng.	12
Tāngmǔ:	Hǎo, xièxie.	13
Fúwùyuán:	Diànlíng zài zhèr,	14
	yǒu shì, suíshí jiào wǒ hǎole.	15

B. DIALOG: SIMPLIFIED CHARACTERS

汤姆：　　对不起，我是汤姆·格林。　　　　　　　　1

服务员：　您好。　　　　　　　　　　　　　　　　2

汤姆：　　旅行社给我们定了房间了吗？　　　　　　3

服务员：　定了。　　　　　　　　　　　　　　　　4
　　　　　这是钥匙——四号房间。　　　　　　　5

汤姆：　　餐厅在哪里？　　　　　　　　　　　　　6

服务员：　中餐厅还是西餐厅？　　　　　　　　　　7

汤姆：　　中餐厅。　　　　　　　　　　　　　　　8

服务员：　在一楼。　　　　　　　　　　　　　　　9

汤姆：　　出租汽车怎么叫的？　　　　　　　　　　10

服务员：　叫汽车　　　　　　　　　　　　　　　　11
　　　　　跟服务台说一下就行。　　　　　　　　12

汤姆：　　好，谢谢。　　　　　　　　　　　　　　13

服务员：　电铃在这儿，　　　　　　　　　　　　　14
　　　　　有事，随时叫我好了。　　　　　　　　15

C. Dialog: Yale Transcription

Tāngmǔ:	Dwèibuchǐ, wǒ shr̀ Tāngmǔ Gélín.	1
Fúwùywán:	Nín hǎu.	2
Tāngmǔ:	Lyǔsyíng shè gěi wǒmen dìngle fángjyān le ma?	3
Fúwùywán:	Dìngle.	4
	Jèi shr̀ yàushr. Sz̀ hǎu fángjyān.	5
Tāngmǔ:	Tsāntīng dzài nǎlǐ?	6
Fúwùywán:	Jūng tsāntīng háishr syī tsāntīng?	7
Tāngmǔ:	Jūng tsāntīng.	8
Fúwùywán:	Dzài yī lóu.	9
Tāngmǔ:	Chūzū chìchē dzěmme jyàude?	10
Fúwùywán:	Jyàu chìchē	11
	gēn fúwù tái shwō yisyà jyòu syíng.	12
Tāngmǔ:	Hǎu, syèsye.	13
Fúwùywán:	Dyànlíng dzài jèr,	14
	yǒu shr̀, swéishŕ jyàu wǒ hǎule.	15

D. DIALOG: FULL CHARACTERS

湯姆：	對不起，我是湯姆‧格林。	1
服務員：	您好。	2
湯姆：	旅行社給我們定房間了嗎？	3
服務員：	定了。	4
	這是鑰匙 —— 四號房間。	5
湯姆：	餐廳在哪裏？	6
服務員：	中餐廳還是西餐廳？	7
湯姆：	中餐廳。	8
服務員：	在一樓。	9
湯姆：	出租汽車怎麼叫的？	10
服務員：	叫汽車	11
	跟服務台説一下就行。	12
湯姆：	好，謝謝。	13
服務員：	電鈴在這兒，	14
	有事，隨時叫我好了。	15

E. Dialog: Vocabulary and Notes

服务
fúwù
To serve.

服务员
fúwù yuán
Attendant, anyone
who serves.

房间
fángjiān
A room.

订房间
dìng fángjiān
To reserve a room.

钥匙
yào·shí
A key.

号
hào
Number, mark, date.

餐厅
cāntīng
A dining hall in a
hotel, a large
restaurant.

楼
lóu
Building; a floor or
story of a building.

服务台
fúwù tái
Service desk.

电铃
diànlíng
Electric bell.

随时
suíshí
At any time you
like.

F. Dialog: English

Tom:	Excuse me. I'm Tom Green.	1
Clerk:	How are you?	2
Tom:	Did the Travel Service reserve a room for us?	3
Clerk:	Yes.	4
	Here's the key. Room number 4.	5
Tom:	Where's the dining room?	6
Clerk:	The Chinese or the Western dining room?	7
Tom:	The Chinese.	8
Clerk:	It's on the first floor.	9
Tom:	How can I call a taxi?	10
Clerk:	To call a car	11
	just ask at the service desk.	12
Tom:	Thank you.	13
Clerk:	The bell is right here.	14
	If you want anything, call me at any time.	15

G. SUBSTITUTIONS: FULL CHARACTERS AND ENGLISH

1. 餐廳　　　　在哪裏？　　　　　　問詢處
   經理辦公室　　　　　　　　　　　廁所

   Where's the <u>dining room</u>?   information desk
   　　　　　manager's office   toilet

2. 對不起，我還要一條毛巾
   　　　　　　　杯冰水
   　　　　　　　瓶熱水
   　　　　　　　塊肥皂
   　　　　　　　瓶啤酒
   　　　　　　　條香烟
   　　　　　　　盒火柴
   　　　　　　　條毯子
   　　　　　　　瓶橘子水

   Excuse me, I want one more <u>towel</u>.
   　　　　　　　cup of ice water
   　　　　　　　bottle of hot water
   　　　　　　　bar of soap
   　　　　　　　bottle of beer
   　　　　　　　pack of cigarettes
   　　　　　　　box of matches
   　　　　　　　blanket
   　　　　　　　bottle of orange juice

H. Substitutions: Simplified Characters and Pinyin

1. 餐厅　　　在哪里 ?　　　　　问询处
经理办公室　　　　　　　　　厕所

   <u>Cāntīng</u>　　　zài nǎlǐ?　　　wènxúnchù
   jīnglǐ bàngōngshì　　　　　　cèsuǒ

2. 对不起，我还要一条毛巾。
杯冰水
瓶热水
块肥皂
瓶啤酒
条香烟
盒火柴
条毯子
瓶桔子水

   Duìbuqǐ, wǒ hái yào yi <u>tiáo máojīn</u>.
   　　　　　　　　　　　bēi bīngshuǐ
   　　　　　　　　　　　píng rèshuǐ
   　　　　　　　　　　　kuài féizào
   　　　　　　　　　　　píng píjiǔ
   　　　　　　　　　　　tiáo xiāngyān
   　　　　　　　　　　　hé huǒchái
   　　　　　　　　　　　tiáo tǎnzi
   　　　　　　　　　　　píng júzi shuǐ

G (2)

3.

這是鑰匙.   電鈴在這兒.

　　毛巾   電梯

　　肥皂   酒巴

　　茶杯   咖啡館

Here's the key.   The electric bell is here.
      a towel   elevator
      some soap   bar
      a tea cup   coffee shop

4.

出租汽車怎麼叫的？   房間 .... 定

飛機票   買   房子 .... 租

How do I call a taxi?   reserve···a room
         buy   an airplane ticket   rent ···· a room

5.

請把這些衣服　洗乾净。

　　這條褲子　燙一燙

　　這雙皮鞋　擦一擦

　　這些行李　搬出去

Please get these clothes   washed.
       get this pair of pants   pressed
       get this pair of shoes   shined
       take these suitcases   out

H (2)

3. 这是钥匙。   电铃 在这儿。

     毛巾   电梯

     肥皂   酒巴

     茶杯   咖啡馆

Zhèi shì <u>yào·shí</u>.   <u>Diànlíng</u> zài zhèr.
    máojīn   diàntī
    féizào   jiǔ bā
    chá bēi   kāfēi guǎn

4. <u>出租汽车</u>怎么<u>叫</u>的？   房间 .... 定

    飞机票   买   房子 .... 租

<u>Chūzū qìchē</u> zěmme <u>jiào</u> de?   fángjiān ··· dìng
<u>fēijī piào</u>   mai   fángzi   ··· zū

5. 请把<u>这些 衣服</u>   <u>洗干净</u>，

     这条裤子   烫一烫

     这双皮鞋   擦一擦

     这些行李   搬出去

Qǐng bǎ <u>zhèixiē yī·fú</u>   <u>xǐ gān·jìng</u>.
    zhèitiáo kùzi   tàng yi tang
    zhèishuāng píxié   cā yi cā
    zhèixiē xínglǐ   bān chūqu

I. Mini Dialogs: Full Characters and English

1.
A. 對不起，我還要幾條毛巾。

B. 行。

A. Excuse me, I want a few more towels.
B. Yes, sir.

2.
A. 我明天一早要走。
請打電話叫醒我。

B. 行。幾點鐘？

A. 五點半。

A. I'm leaving early tomorrow.
Please give me a call.
B. Yes sir. What time?
A. Five thirty.

3.
A. 中國的電壓是多少？

B. 220伏。

A. 頻率呢？

B. 50週。

A. How much is the voltage in China?
B. 220 volts.
A. And the frequency?
B. 50 cycles.

J. Mini Dialogs: Simplified Characters and Pinyin

1.
> A. 对不起，我还要几条毛巾。
>
> B. 行。
>
> A. Duìbuqǐ, wǒ hái yào jǐ tiáo máojīn.
> B. Xíng.

2.
> A. 我明天一早要走。
>   请打电话叫醒我。
>
> B. 行，几点钟？
>
> A. 五点半。
>
> A. Wǒ míngtiān yi zǎo yào zǒu.
>   Qǐng dǎ diànhuà jiàoxǐng wǒ.
> B. Xíng. Jǐ diǎnzhōng?
> A. Wǔ diǎn bàn.

3.
> A. 中国的电压是多少？
>
> B. 220 伏。
>
> A. 频率呢？
>
> B. 50 周。
>
> A. Zhōngguode diànyā shì duōshǎo?
> B. Èrbǎi èrshi fú.
> A. Pínlǜ ne?
> B. Wǔshi zhōu.

I (2)

4.
A. 這房間真冷。
暖氣壞了。
經理辦公室在哪兒？
我要去提意見。
B. 就在那兒。

A. This room's awfully cold.
The radiator isn't working.
Where's the manager's office?
I want to make a complaint.
B. It's over there.

5.
A. 請把這些衣服洗干淨燙好。
B. 行。甚麼時候要？
A. 十點以前。
B. 行。

A. Please have these clothes cleaned and pressed.
B. Yes sir. When do you want them?
A. By 10 o'clock.
B. Yes sir.

条	tiáo Classifier for towels.	毛巾	máojīn Towel.	一早	yi zǎo Early.
伏	fú Volts.	頻率	pínlǜ Frequency.	周	zhōu Cycles.
洗	xǐ To wash.			干净	gān.jìng Clean.

J (2)

4.
A. 这房间真冷。
　　暖气坏了。
　　经理办公室在哪儿？
　　我要去提意见。
B. 就在那儿。

A. Zhèi fángjiān zhēn lěng.
　Nuǎnqì huàile.
　Jīnglǐ bàngōngshì zài nǎr?
　Wǒ yào qù tí yìjian.
B. Jiù zài nàr.

5.
A. 请把这些衣服洗干净烫好。
B. 行。什么时候要？
A. 十点以前。
B. 行。

A. Qǐng bǎ zhèixie yīfu xǐ gānjing tàng hǎo.
　B. Xíng.　Shémme shíhòu yào?
A. Shí diǎn yǐqián.
　B. Xíng.

叫醒	jiàoxǐng To awaken.	电压	diànyā Voltage.
暖气	nuǎnqì Central heating.	经理	jīnglǐ Manager.
提意见	tí yì·jiàn To complain.	烫(衣服)	tàng (yīfu) To iron, press.

K. CULTURAL NOTES

Chinese hotels. The big hotels in China's cities are the best places for taking care of foreigners' needs. Not only will they always have a Western dining room in addition to the Chinese dining room, but they can also usually arrange for special kinds of dietary requirements.

Chinese hosts usually offer their guests hot drinks. And hotel rooms will usually have a thermos with hot water instead of cold water (lěng shuǐ[a]) and ice cubes (bīngkuài[b]). But any guest who wants iced drinks needs only to ask. There is usually no problem in getting cold drinks—it's just that the Chinese consider it impolite to *offer* them (hot drinks show the warmth of the welcome).

Chinese food. There are four main schools of Chinese cooking.

1. Sichuan food (Sìchuān[c]) specializes in hot and spicy food.
2. Cantonese food (Guǎngdōng[d]) specializes in crisp, lightly cooked vegetables and a wide variety of delicate flavors.
3. Shanghai food (Jiāngsū[e] and Zhèjiang[f]) specializes in fragrance and color and tends to be slightly sweet.
4. Shandong food (Shāndōng[g]) is known for being very simple and non-greasy.

Some of the best-known dishes from various parts of China are listed below.

1. Roast Peking duck (Běijīng kǎo yā[h]).
2. Cantonese roast suckling pig (Guǎngzhōu kǎo rǔ zhū[i]).
3. Chengdu's Mapo bean curd (Chéngdū Mápó dòufu[j]).
4. Hangzhou's sweet and sour Westlake fish (Hángzhōu xīhú tángcù yú[k]).

a. 冷水	d. 广东	h. 北京烤鸭
b. 冰块	e. 江苏	i. 广州烤乳猪
c. 四川	f. 浙江	j. 成都麻婆豆腐
	g. 山东	k. 杭州西湖糖醋鱼

LESSON 17

ASKING DIRECTIONS

问 路

A. Dialog: Pinyin Transcription

| Ānnā: | Duìbuqǐ, wǒ mǐ lù le. | 1 |

| Mòshēngrén: | Nǐ yào dào nǎr qù ya? | 2 |

| Ānnā: | Dào guójì lǚguǎn, zěmme zǒu a? | 3 |

Mòshēngrén:	Ràng wǒ xiǎngxiang.	4
	Nǐ xiān yi zhí zǒu,	5
	jiàn dào dì yīge hónglùdēng wǎng yòu guǎi,	6
	zài wǎng qián zǒu yi tiáo jiē, zài ···	7

Ānnā:	Āyà! Qǐng jiǎng màn yi diǎr.	8
	Wǒde Zhōngwén bu tài hǎo.	9
	Nǐ shuō de wǒ bu dǒng.	10
	Haih![1] Zěmme bàn ne?[2]	11

| Mòshēngrén: | Zhèi yàng ba. Nǐ gēn wǒ zǒu ba. | 12 |

| Ānnā: | Nǐ yě qù guójì lǚguǎn ma? | 13 |

| Mòshēngrén: | Bú shi. | 14 |
| | Dàn shi, wǒ yě qù nèige fāngxiàng. | 15 |

| Ānnā: | Nà tài hǎole. Qiǎo jí le. | 16 |

B. DIALOG: SIMPLIFIED CHARACTERS

安娜: 对不起，我迷路了。   1

陌生人: 你要到哪儿去呀？   2

安娜: 到国际旅馆，怎么走啊？   3

陌生人: 让我想想。   4
           你先一直走，   5
           见到第一个红绿灯往右拐，   6
           再往前走一条街，再…   7

安娜: 啊呀！请讲慢一点儿。   8
           我的中文不太好。   9
           你说的我不懂。   10
           咳[1]！怎么办呢？[2]   11

陌生人: 这样吧，你跟我走吧。   12

安娜: 你也去国际旅馆吗？   13

陌生人: 不是。   14
           但是，我也去那个方向。   15

安娜: 那太好了，巧极了。   16

C. Dialog: Yale Transcription.

| Ānnā: | Dwèibuchǐ, wǒ mǐ lù le. | 1 |

Mwòshēngrén: Nǐ yàu dàu nǎr chyù ya?   2

Ānnā: Dàu gwójì lyǔgwǎn, dzěmme dzǒu a?   3

Mwòshēngrén: Ràng wǒ syǎngsyang.   4

              Nǐ syān yi jř dzǒu,   5

              jyàn dàu dì yīge húnglyùdēng wǎng yòu gwǎi,   6

              dzài wǎng chyán dzǒu yi tyáu jyē, dzài ···   7

Ānnā: Āyà! Chǐng jyǎng màn yi dyǎr.   8

              Wǒde Jūngwén bu tài hǎu.   9

              Nǐ shwō de wǒ bu dǔng.   10

              Haih!¹ Dzěmme bàn ne?²   11

Mwòshēngrén: Jèi yàng ba. Nǐ gēn wǒ dzǒu ba.   12

Ānnā: Nǐ yě chyù gwójì lyǔgwǎn ma?   13

Mwòshēngrén: Bú shr.   14

              Dàn shr, wǒ yě chyù nèige fāngsyàng.   15

Ānna: Nà tài hǎule. Chiǎu jí le.   16

D. DIALOG: FULL CHARACTERS

安娜：	對不起，我迷路了。	1
陌生人：	你要到哪兒去呀？	2
安娜：	到國際旅館，怎麼走啊？	3
陌生人：	讓我想想。	4
	你先一直走，	5
	見到第一個紅綠燈往右拐，	6
	再往前走一條街，再…	7
安娜：	啊呀！請講慢一點兒。	8
	我的中文不太好。	9
	你說的我不懂。	10
	咳[1]！怎麼辦呢[2]？	11
陌生人：	這樣吧，你跟我走吧。	12
安娜：	你也去國際旅館嗎？	13
陌生人：	不是。	14
	但是，我也去那個方向。	15
安娜：	那太好了，巧極了。	16

E. Dialog: Vocabulary and Notes

陌生人　mòshēngrén
　　　　A stranger.

问路　wèn lù
　　　To ask directions
　　　(to ask the road
　　　or way).

迷路　mí lù
　　　To lose one's way.

国际　guójì
　　　International.

灯　dēng
　　Light, lamp.

红　hóng
　　Red.

绿　lǜ
　　Green.

红绿灯　hónglǜ dēng
　　　　Traffic light.

往　wàng
　　Toward, in the di-
　　rection of.

拐　guǎi
　　To turn.

条　tiáo
　　Classifier for
　　streets.

一条街　yi tiáo jiē
　　　　One street, one
　　　　block.

办　bàn
　　To do, manage,
　　carry out, handle.

方向　fāngxiàng
　　　Direction.

1. <u>haih</u>.[a]　The whole syllable is voiceless: a breathy sigh.

2. <u>zěmme bàn ne?</u>[b]　This is said under her breath. She is talking
   to herself (or at least trying to give the impression that she
   is talking to herself). It would be presumptuous to really
   ask this of a stranger.

　　a. 咳　　　　　　　　b. 怎么办呢？

F. Dialog: English

Anna: Excuse me. I've lost my way.   1

Stranger: Where do you want to go?   2

Anna: How do you get to the International Hotel?   3

Stranger: Let me think.   4

           First go straight ahead.   5

           When you get to the first traffic light, turn right.   6

           Then go straight ahead one block, and then ···   7

Anna: Wait a minute. Please speak slower.   8

           My Chinese isn't too good.   9

           I can't follow you.   10

           Oh gee. What can I do?   11

Stranger: Why don't you walk along with me?   12

Anna: Are you going to the International Hotel, too?   13

Stranger: No,   14

           but I'm going in that direction.   15

Anna: Oh, great! How lucky!   16

G. Substitutions: Full Characters and English

1. 請講慢一點兒。   大聲
    清楚   小聲

   Please speak a little <u>slower</u>.   louder
                        more clearly   softer

2. 到國際旅館，怎麼 走 ?
    上海電影院   找
    這個地址
    這個醫院

   How do I <u>get to</u> the <u>International Hotel</u>?
            find   Shanghai Theater
                           this address
                           this hospital

3. 見到第一個紅綠燈往右拐。
    第二個路口   左
    第三條街
    一座高樓

   When you get to <u>the first traffic light</u>, turn <u>right</u>.
                   the corner   left
                   the third street
                   a tall building

H. SUBSTITUTIONS: SIMPLIFIED CHARACTERS AND PINYIN

---

1. 请讲<u>慢</u>一点儿 。　　　　大声
　　清楚　　　　　　　　　　小声

Qǐng jiǎng <u>màn</u>　　yi diǎr.　　　　dà shēng
　　　　qīng•chǔ　　　　　　　　xiǎo shēng

---

2. 到<u>国际旅馆</u>，　<u>怎么走</u> ?
　上海电影院　　　找
　这个地址
　这个医院

Dào <u>guójì lǚguǎn</u>　　　<u>zěmme zǒu</u>?
　Shànghai diànyǐngyuàn　　zhǎo
　zhèige dìzhǐ
　zhèige yīyuàn

---

3. 见到<u>第一个红绿灯</u>往<u>右</u>拐 。
　　第二个路口　　左
　　第三条街
　　一座高楼

Jiàn dào <u>dìyī ge hónglǜ dēng</u>　wǎng <u>yòu</u> guǎi.
　　dì èr ge lùkou　　　　　　zuǒ
　　dì sān tiáo jiē
　　yi zuò gāo lóu

I. Mini Dialogs: Full Characters and English

1.
A. 渴死了。哪兒有水喝？

B. 這兒有水。

A. I'm dying of thirst. Where can I get some water?
B. Here's some water.

2.
A. 對不起，男廁所在哪兒？

B. 上樓，往左拐，
你就能看到了。

A. Excuse me, where's the men's room?
B. Go upstairs and turn left.
You'll see it there.

3.
A. 請問，這個地址怎麼找？

B. 對不起，我才到這裏。

A. 沒關係。

A. May I ask you how I can find this address?
B. I'm sorry, I'm a newcomer here.
A. That's all right.

厕所   cèsuǒ
Toilet.

上楼   shànglóu
To go upstairs.

J. MINI DIALOGS: SIMPLIFIED CHARACTERS AND PINYIN

1.
A. 渴死了，哪儿有水喝？

B. 这儿有水。

A. Kěsǐle. Nǎr yǒu shuǐ hē?
B. Zhèr yǒu shuǐ.

2.
A. 对不起，男厕所在哪儿？

B. 上楼，往左拐，
你就能看到了。

A. Duìbuqǐ, nán cèsuǒ zài nǎr?
B. Shànglóu, wǎng zuǒ guǎi,
nǐ jiù néng kàn dàole.

3.
A. 请问，这个地址怎么找？

B. 对不起，我才到这里。

A. 没关系。

A. Qǐng wèn, zhèige dìzhǐ zěmme zhǎo?
B. Duìbuqǐ, wǒ cái dào zhèilǐ.
A. Méi guānxi.

地址   dìzhǐ
Address.

I (2)

4.
A. 對不起，女廁所在哪裏？

B. 就在那兒，看見了嗎？
門上貼了一個女人頭象。

A. 喔，看見了。

A. Excuse me, where's the ladies' room?
  B. Over there. See it?
    There's an image of a woman's head on the door.
A. Oh, I see it.

5.
A. 請問，
到上海電影院怎麽走？

B. 呣…，從這兒一直走，
過三個路口就到了。

A. 對不起，
請再說一遍，慢慢兒的。

A. May I ask you
  how to get to the Shanghai Theater?
  B. Let's see. Go straight ahead from here.
    Go three blocks and you'll be there.
A. Excuse me.
  Please say that again, slowly.

才   cái
     Just, only.

貼   tiē
     To stick on.

路口 lùkǒu
     The entrance to a street.

一遍 yibiàn
     One time.

J (2)

4.
A. 对不起，女厕所在哪里？

   B. 就在那儿，看见了吗？
      门上贴了一个女人头象。

A. 喔，看见了。

A. Duìbuqǐ, nǚ cèsuǒ zài nǎlǐ.
　B. Jiù zài nàr, kànjianle ma?
　　　Ménshàng tiēle yige nǚrén tóu xiàng.
A. Ò, kànjianle.

5.
A. 请问，
   到上海电影院怎么走？

   B. 嗯…，从这儿一直走，
      过三个路口就到了。

A. 对不起，
   请再说一遍，慢慢儿的。

A. Qǐng wèn,
　　dào Shànghǎi diànyǐng yuàn zěmme zǒu?
　B. Mmm… cóng zhèr yizhí zǒu,
　　　guò sānge lùkǒu jiù dàole.
A. Duìbuqǐ,
　　qǐng zài shuō yibiàn, mànmārde.

头象　tóu xiàng
The image of a head.

电影院　diànyǐng yuàn
A movie theater.

K. CULTURAL NOTES

Addressing strangers. In the early 1950s, tóngzhì[a] (comrade) largely replaced the many different traditional ways of addressing strangers, as a means of showing equality among the people. But during the 1960s the use of this word started to decline—and without any convenient replacement. The situation now is similar to English, which also lacks a term with which to call strangers. The speaker simply attracts the stranger's attention with 'Excuse me' (duìbuqi[b]) or 'May I ask you something?' (qǐng wèn[c]).

a. 同志   b. 对不起   c. 请问

LESSON 18

TRAVELING IN CHINA

在 中 国 旅 行

A. Dialog: Pinyin Transcription

Lǎoshī: Tāngmǔ, Ānnā, nǐmen lǚxíng gāng huí lái ba.   1

Tāngmǔ: Duì, gāng huí lái.   2

Lǎoshī: Wán de hěn hǎo ba.   3

Ānnā: Hěn hǎo hěn hǎo.   4

Lǎoshī: Zhèi táng kè shang   5

         qǐng nǐmen tántan zài Zhōngguo lǚxíng, hǎo ma?   6

Tāngmǔ: Hǎo a.   7

Ānnā: Zhèi cì lǚxíng a,   8

         wǒmen shì wěituō Zhōngguo lǚxíng shè ānpái de.   9

Tāngmǔ: Wǒmen dàole Shànghǎi, Nánjīng, Guìlín.   10

Lǎoshī: Yidìng cānguānle bu shǎo míngshèng gǔjì ba.   11

Ānnā: À, Zhōngguode míngshèng gǔjì zhēn bu shǎo.   12

Lǎoshī: Jiùshi a.   13

         Duìle, nǐmen zuòde shì fēijī háishi huǒchē?   14

Ānnā: Dōu zuòle.   15

Tāngmǔ: Wǒmen duì zhèi cì lǚxíng shì fēicháng mǎnyì de.   16

B. DIALOG: SIMPLIFIED CHARACTERS

老师: 汤姆、安娜，你们旅行刚回来吧。   1

汤姆: 对，刚回来。   2

老师: 玩得很好吧。   3

安娜: 很好很好。   4

老师: 这堂课上   5
      请你们谈谈在中国旅行，好吗？   6

汤姆: 好啊。   7

安娜: 这次旅行啊，   8
      我们是委托中国旅行社安排的。   9

汤姆: 我们到了上海、南京、桂林。   10

老师: 一定参观了不少名胜古迹吧。   11

安娜: 啊！中国的名胜古迹真不少。   12

老师: 就是啊。   13
      对了，你们坐的是飞机还是火车？   14

安娜: 都坐了。   15

汤姆: 我们对这次旅行是非常满意的。   16

C. Dialog: Yale Transcription

Lǎushr̄: Tāngmǔ, Ānnā, nǐmen lyǔsyíng gāng hwéi lái ba.   1

Tāngmǔ: Dwèi, gāng hwéi lái.   2

Lǎushr̄: Wán de hěn hǎu ba.   3

Ānnā: Hěn hǎu hěn hǎu.   4

Lǎushr̄: Jèi táng kè shang   5

          chǐng nǐmen tántan dzài Jūnggwo lyǔsyíng, hǎu ma?   6

Tāngmǔ: Hǎu a.   7

Ānnā: Jèi tsż lyǔsyíng a,   8

          wǒmen shr̀ wěitwō Jūnggwo lyǔshíng shè ānpái de.   9

Tāngmǔ: Wǒmen dàule Shànghǎi, Nánjīng, Gwèilín.   10

Lǎushr̄: Yidǐng tsāngwānle bu shǎu míngshèng gǔjì ba.   11

Ānnā: À, Jūnggwode míngshèng gǔjì jēn bu shǎu.   12

Lǎushr̄: Jyòushr a.   13

          Dwèile, nǐmen dzwòde shr̀ fēijī háishr hwǒchē?   14

Ānnā: Dōu dzwòle.   15

Tāngmǔ: Wǒmen dwèi jèi tsż lyǔsyíng shr̀ fēicháng mǎnyì de.   16

D. DIALOG: FULL CHARACTERS

老師：湯姆、安娜，你們旅行剛回來吧。   1

湯姆：對，剛回來。   2

老師：玩得很好吧。   3

安娜：很好很好。   4

老師：這堂課上   5
       請你們談談在中國旅行，好嗎？   6

湯姆：好啊。   7

安娜：這次旅行啊，   8
       我們是委托中國旅行社安排的。   9

湯姆：我們到了上海、南京、桂林。   10

老師：一定參觀了不少名勝古蹟吧。   11

安娜：啊！中國的名勝古蹟真不少。   12

老師：就是啊。   13
       對了，你們坐的是飛機還是火車？   14

安娜：都坐了。   15

湯姆：我們對這次旅行是非常滿意的。   16

E. Dialog: Vocabulary and Notes

玩　wán
To play, have fun, enjoy.

一堂课　yi táng kè
A class period.
(<u>táng</u> is a classifier.)

谈　tán
To discuss, talk.

参观　cānguān
To visit a place.

名胜　míng shèng
Places of scenic or historic interest.

古迹　gǔ jì
Historic spots, ruins.

对(于)　duì (yu)
Concerning, with regard to.

满意　mǎnyì
To be satisfied with.

F. DIALOG: ENGLISH

Teacher: Tom, Anna, you've just returned from your trip.   1

Tom: Yes, we have.   2

Teacher: I trust you enjoyed yourselves.   3

Anna: Yes, indeed.   4

Teacher: During this class   5

          could you talk about 'Traveling in China'?   6

Tom: Sure.   7

Anna: This trip, you know,   8

          was arranged by the China Travel Service.   9

Tom: We got as far as Shanghai, Nanjing, and Guilin.   10

Teacher: You must have visited lots of scenic spots and   11
          historic sites.

Anna: Yes. China has plenty of them.   12

Teacher: Quite right.   13

          By the way, did you go by plane, or train?   14

Anna: Both.   15

Tom: We couldn't have been more satisfied with the trip.   16

G. Substitutions: Full Characters and English

---

1. 到過中國的<u>北部</u>。

   東北   西北
   南方   中部

   We've been to the <u>North</u>   of China.
   　　　　　　　　　Northeast   Northwest
   　　　　　　　　　South   central part

---

2. 請你們談談<u>在中國旅行</u>，怎麼樣？
   　　　　怎麼做中國菜
   　　　　學中文的經驗

   How about telling us about <u>your travels in China?</u>
   　　　　　　　　　　　　　　how to cook Chinese food
   　　　　　　　　　　　　　　your experience learning Chinese

---

3. <u>票</u>　已經<u>訂好</u>了。

   菜　　　　點
   旅行　　　結束
   功課　　　做完

   I've already <u>booked</u>   <u>the tickets.</u>
   　　　　　　ordered   the dishes
   　　　　　　completed   my travels
   　　　　　　finished doing   my homework

H. Substitutions: Simplified Characters and Pinyin

---

1. 到过中国的 <u>北部</u> 。

      东北   西北

      南方   中部

Dào•guò Zhōngguo de <u>běibù</u>.
          dōngbei   xīběi
          nánfāng   zhōngbù

---

2. 请你们谈谈 <u>在中国旅行</u> ，   怎么样？

             怎么做中国菜

             学中文的经验

Qǐng nǐmen tántan <u>Zài Zhōngguo lǚxíng</u> , zěmme yàng?
                Zěmme zuò Zhōngguo cài
                Xué Zhōngwén de jīngyàn

---

3. <u>票</u>   已经订好了 。

  菜   点

  旅行   结束

  功课   做完

<u>Piào</u> yǐjīng <u>dìng hǎo</u> le.
cài   diǎn
lǚxíng   jiéshù
gōngkè   zuò wán

I. MINI DIALOGS: FULL CHARACTERS AND ENGLISH

1.
A. 到中國多久了？
B. 一個星期了。
A. 到過哪些地方呀？
B. 到過中國的北部。
現在正在北京游覽，
明天要到上海去。

A. How long have you been in China?
B. One week.
A. What places have you been to?
B. I've been to the Northern part.
Right now I'm sightseeing in Peking.
Tomorrow I'm going to Shanghai.

2.
A. 坐火車去還是坐飛機去？
B. 坐飛機去。
票已經訂好了。

A. Are you going by train or plane?
B. By plane.
I've already booked a ticket.

北部　běi bù　The Northern part.

游览　yóu lǎn　To go sightseeing.

J. Mini Dialogs: Simplified Characters and Pinyin

1. A. 到中国多久了？
    B. 一个星期了。
    A. 到过哪些地方呀？
    B. 到过中国的北部，
       现在正在北京游览，
       明天要到上海去。

    A. Dào Zhōngguo duō jiǔ le?
      B. Yīge xīngqi le.
    A. Dàoguo něixiē dìfang ya?
      B. Dàoguo Zhōngguode běi bù.
        Xiànzài zhèngzài Běijīng yóulǎn.
        Míngtiān yào dào Shànghǎi qù.

2. A. 坐火车去还是坐飞机去？
    B. 坐飞机去。
       票已经订好了。

    A. Zuò huǒchē qù háishi zuò fēijī qù?
      B. Zuò fēijī qù.
        Piào yǐjīng dìng hǎole.

票   piào
    Ticket.

订   dìng
    To make a reservation.

I (2)

3.
A. 你是甚麼時候來中國的？

B. 九月初，你呢？

A. 前天．

你從哪兒入境的？

B. 北京．

A. When did you come to China?
  B. In early September. And you?
A. The day before yesterday.
  Where did you enter the country?
  B. Peking.

4.
A. 你從哪兒出境呢？

B. 從廣州．

我從廣州坐火車到香港，

再從香港到日本．

A. 嗬，你安排得可真好啊。

A. Where are you going to leave the country from?
  B. From Canton.
    From Canton I'm taking a train to Hong Kong.
    And from Hong Kong I'm going to Japan.
A. Boy, you've really arranged things well.

初   chū
     The first part of.

前天   qiántiān
       The day before
       yesterday.

可真好 is a little stronger than 真好．

J (2)

3.
A. 你是什么时候来中国的？

B. 九月初。你呢？

A. 前天。

你从哪儿入境的？

B. 北京，

A. Nǐ shì shémme shíhou lái Zhōngguo de?
B. Jiǔ yuè chū. Nǐ ne?
A. Qián tiān.
   Nǐ cóng nǎr rù jìng de?
B. Běijīng.

4.
A. 你从哪儿出境呢？

B. 从广州。

我从广州坐火车到香港，

再从香港到日本。

A. 嘀！你安排得可真好啊。

A. Nǐ cóng nǎr chū jìng ne?
B. Cóng Guǎngzhōu.
   Wǒ cóng Guǎngzhōu zuò huǒchē dào Xiānggǎng.
   Zài cóng Xiānggǎng dào Rìběn.
A. Hē! Nǐ ānpái de kě zhēn hǎo a.

入境　rù jìng
To enter a border.

出境　chū jìng
To exit a border.

K. Cultural Notes

Map of China. The following map shows the provinces of China in pinyin transcription. The tones aren't shown, and the province of Shǎnxi is spelled Shaanxi to distinguish it from Shānxi. The map is taken from *China: A General Survey,* by Qi Wen (Beijing: Foreign Languages Press, 1981).

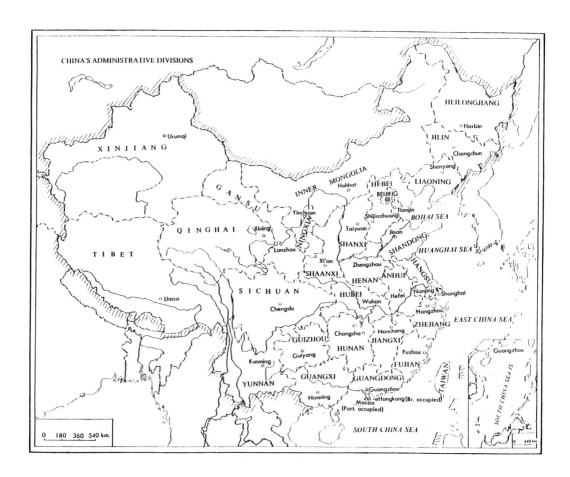

LESSON 19

HOW DID THEY LEARN CHINESE?

总 结 经 验

A. Dialog: Pinyin Transcription

Lǎoshī:	Tāngmǔ, Ānnā,	1
	nǐmen jiǎng Zhōngguo huà de nénglì	2
	tígāo de zhēn kuài ya.	3
Ānnā:	Nà shì yīnwei lǎoshī jiāo de hǎo a.	4
Lǎoshī:	Zhǔyào háishi nǐmen zìjǐ de nǔlì.	5
	Wǒ xīwàng nǐmen zǒngjié yixià jīngyàn.[1]	6
Tāngmǔ:	Wǒ juéde kāishǐ shí,	7
	yào zhǎngwò hǎo sì shēng hé qīngzhòng yīn.	8
Ānnā:	Yào duō liàn duō jiǎng.	9
Tāngmǔ:	Hái yào lìyòng lùyīnjī.	10
Ānnā:	Dànshi zuìzui zhòngyàode	11
	háishi yào zài Zhōngguo zhù yi duàn shíjiān.	12
	Tāngmǔ, nǐ shuō ne?	13
Tāngmǔ:	Nà dāngrán luo.	14
	Dànshi, wǒmen de xiě háishi buxíng.	15
	Huíguó yǐhòu hái děi jìxu xuéxi.	16

B. DIALOG: SIMPLIFIED CHARACTERS

老师: 汤姆、安娜，   1
你们讲中国话的能力   2
提高得真快呀。   3

安娜: 那是因为老师教得好啊。   4

老师: 主要还是你们自己的努力。   5
我希望你们总结一下经验[1]。   6

汤姆: 我觉得开始时   7
要掌握好四声和轻重音。   8

安娜: 要多练、多讲。   9

汤姆: 还要利用录音机。   10

安娜: 但是，最最重要的   11
还是要在中国住一段时间。   12
汤姆，你说呢？   13

汤姆: 那当然啰。   14
但是，我们的写还是不行。   15
回国以后还得继续学习。   16

C. Dialog: Yale Transcription

Lǎushr̄:	Tāngmǔ, Ānnā,	1
	nǐmen jyǎng Jūnggwo hwà de nénglì	2
	tígāu de jēn kwài ya.	3
Ānnā:	Nà shr̀ yīnwei lǎushr̄ jyāu de hǎu a.	4
Lǎushr̄:	Jǔyàu háishr nǐmen dz̀jǐ de nǔlì.	5
	Wǒ syīwàng nǐmen dzǔngjyé yisyà jīngyàn.[1]	6
Tāngmǔ:	Wǒ jywéde kāishr̄ shŕ,	7
	yàu jǎng-wǒ hǎu sz̀ shēng hé chīngjùng yīn.	8
Ānnā:	Yàu dwō lyàn dwō jyǎng.	9
Tāngmǔ:	Hái yàu lìyùng lùyīnjī.	10
Ānnā:	Dànshr dzwèidzwei jùngyàude	11
	háishr yàu dzài Jūnggwo jù yi dwàn shŕjyān.	12
	Tāngmǔ, nǐ shwō ne?	13
Tāngmǔ:	Nà dāngrán lwo.	14
	Dànshr, wǒmen de syě háishr busyíng.	15
	Hwéigwó yǐhòu hái děi jìsyù sywésyi.	16

D. DIALOG: FULL CHARACTERS

老師：湯姆、安娜，   1
　　　你們講中國話的能力   2
　　　提高得真快呀。   3

安娜：那是因為老師教得好啊。   4

老師：主要還是你們自己的努力。   5
　　　我希望你們總結一下經驗[1]。   6

湯姆：我覺得開始時   7
　　　要掌握好四聲和輕重音。   8

安娜：要多練、多講。   9

湯姆：還要利用錄音機。   10

安娜：但是，最最重要的   11
　　　還是要在中國住一段時間。   12
　　　湯姆，你說呢？   13

湯姆：那當然囉。   14
　　　但是，我們的寫還是不行。   15
　　　回國以後還得繼續學習。   16

E. DIALOG: VOCABULARY AND NOTES

经验　jīngyàn
Experience.

能力　nénglì
Ability.

主要　zhǔyào
Main, essential.

努力　nǔlì
Diligence, effort.

总结　zǒngjié
To summarize, distill.

掌握　zhǎngwò
To master.

声　shēng
Sound.

轻　qīng
Light (in weight).

重　zhòng
Heavy.

音　yīn
Sound.

轻重音　qīngzhòng yīn
Word stress.

练　liàn
Practice, drill, train.

利用　lìyòng
To use.

录音　lù yīn
To record sounds.

录音机　lùyīnjī
A tape recorder.

重要　zhòngyào
Important.

段　duàn
A section, portion, piece, period.

当然　dāngrán
Of course.

当然啰　dāngrán luo
Of course! It goes without saying.

1. <u>zǒngjié jīngyàn</u>.[a] 'To learn from experience.' <u>Zǒngjié</u>[b] is more like 'to distill from' or 'to extract from', here, than 'to summarize'. 'To distill the good or bad points from an experience and learn from them.' This phrase is especially common in China today where there is an atmosphere of 'trying out many different approaches to find out which works best.' That is, they try something and then <u>zǒngjié jīngyàn</u>.[a]

   a.　总结经验　　　　b.　总结

F. Dialog: English

Teacher:	Tom, Anna,	1
	your ability in speaking Chinese	2
	has really improved fast.	3
Anna:	That's because you've taught us so well.	4
Teacher:	The important thing has been your own diligence.	5
	I hope you can point out the things that led to your success.	6
Tom:	Well, I feel that from the very start	7
	you should master the four tones and the stress.	8
Anna:	And you should practice a lot and speak a lot.	9
Tom:	And use a tape recorder.	10
Anna:	But the most important thing	11
	is to live for a period of time in China.	12
	What do you say, Tom?	13
Tom:	That goes without saying.	14
	But our writing is still not good enough.	15
	After we get home, we'll have to continue studying it.	16

G. Substitutions: Full Characters and English

1. 要<u>多練多講</u>。
    掌握好四聲
    利用錄音機
    在中國住一段時間

    You should <u>practice a lot and speak a lot.</u>
                master the four tones
                use a tape recorder
                live for a period of time in China

2. <u>囘國</u>以後還得<u>繼續學習</u>。
    畢業   在工作中學習
    吃飯   工作

    After I <u>get back home</u>, I still have to <u>keep studying.</u>
        graduate   study in my work
        eat   work

3. <u>主要</u> 是<u>你們自己的努力</u>。
    <u>其次</u>才是<u>老師教得好</u>。

    <u>Most important</u>   is <u>your own diligence.</u>
    <u>Next to that</u>, then, is <u>the teacher's skill.</u>

H. SUBSTITUTIONS: SIMPLIFIED CHARACTERS AND PINYIN

1. 要多练多讲 。
   掌握好四声
   利用录音机
   在中国住一段时间

   Yào <u>duō liàn duō jiǎng</u>.
   <u>zhǎngwò hǎo sì shēng</u>
   <u>lìyòng lùyīnjī</u>
   <u>zài Zhōngguo zhù yi duàn shíjiān</u>

2. <u>回国</u> 以后还得 <u>继续学习</u> 。
   毕业   在工作中学习
   吃饭   工作

   <u>Huí guó</u> yǐhòu, hái děi <u>jìxù xué·xí</u>.
   <u>bìyè</u>   <u>zài gōngzuò xué·xí</u>
   <u>chīfàn</u>   <u>gōngzuò</u>

3. <u>主要</u>   是 <u>你们自已的努力</u> 。
   <u>其次</u> 才是 <u>老师教得好</u> 。

   <u>Zhǔyào</u>   shì <u>nǐmen zìjǐ de nǔlì</u>.
   <u>Qícì</u> cái shì <u>lǎoshī jiāo de hǎo</u>.

I. Mini Dialogs: Full Characters and English

1.
A. 你的中國話講得真好。
   要是不看你的臉，
   我真會以為是中國人在講話呢。
B. 是嗎？

A. Your Chinese is really excellent.
   If I didn't see your face,
   I'd take you for a Chinese.
B. Really?

2.
A. 你的學習經驗很好啊！
B. 只能供你參考。
A. 你別謙虛了。
B. 我不是謙虛。
   真的！
   各人的情況不一樣，
   我的不一定適合別人的。

A. The ideas from your studying experience are excellent.
   B. I only offer them for your information
A. You shouldn't be so modest.
   B. I'm not being modest.
       It's a fact.
       Different people have different circumstances.
       My ideas aren't necessarily suitable for others.

J. MINI DIALOGS: SIMPLIFIED CHARACTERS AND PINYIN

1.
> A. 你的中国话讲得真好。
>
>   要是不看你的脸，
>
>   我真会以为是中国人在讲话呢。
>
> B. 是吗？
>
> A. Nǐde Zhōngguo huà jiǎng de zhēn hǎo.
>   Yàoshi bu kàn nǐde liǎn,
>   wǒ zhēn huì yǐwei shì Zhōngguo rén zài jiǎng huà ne.
> B. Shì ma?

2.
> A. 你的学习经验很好啊！
>
> B. 只能供你参考。
>
> A. 你别谦虚了。
>
> B. 我不是谦虚。
>
>   真的！
>
>   各人的情况不一样，
>
>   我的不一定适合别人的。
>
> A. Nǐde xuéxi jīngyàn hěn hǎo a!
>   B. Zhǐ néng gòng nǐ cānkǎo.
> A. Nǐ bié qiānxū le.
>   B. Wǒ búshi qiānxū.
>   Zhēnde!
>   Gè rén de qíngkuàng bu yiyàng.
>   Wǒde bu yidìng shìhé bié rénde.

I (2)

3.
A. 你的中文學了幾年？

　B. 五年.

A. 在哪裏學的？

　B. 英國.

　　可是學得不好.

A. How long did you study Chinese?
  B. Five years.
A. Where did you study it?
  B. In England.
     But I didn't learn it well.

4.
A. 學講中國話的經驗，

　你能談談嗎？

　B. 啊呀，談不上有甚麼經驗.

　　只是覺得

　　要掌握四聲，多練多講.

A. This experience of learning to speak Chinese,
   can you say something about it?
  B. Well, it's not really worth talking about.
     I just feel that
     you should master the four tones and practice a lot.

臉　　lián
　　　Face.

以为　　yǐwei
　　　To consider, think.

适合　　shìhé
　　　Be suitable.

J (2)

3.
A. 你的中文学了几年？

   B. 五年。

A. 在哪里学的？

   B. 英国。
      可是学得不好。

A. Nǐde Zhōngwén xuéle jǐ nián.
   B. Wǔ nián.
A. Zài nǎlǐ xuéde?
   B. Yīngguo.
      Kěshì xué de bu hǎo.

4.
A. 学讲中国话的经验，
   你能谈谈吗？

   B. 啊呀，谈不上有什么经验。
      只是觉得
      要掌握四声，多练讲。

A. Xué jiǎng Zhōngguo huà de jīngyàn,
   nǐ néng tántan ma?
   B. Āyà, tán bushàng yǒu shémme jīngyàn.
      Zhǐshi juéde
      yào zhǎngwò sì shēng, duō liàn jiǎng.

| 供 | gòng To offer, supply. | 参考 | cānkǎo To refer, reference. |

谈不上   tán bushàng
Not worth talking about.

K. CULTURAL NOTES

Varieties of Putonghua. It would be unthinkable for a British college professor to lecture in Cockney, or for a United States senator to address the Senate in Brooklynese—even though they would be perfectly well understood. In most languages that have a standard pronunciation (like England), and even in some that don't (like the United States), how a person makes his *sounds* has importance far beyond his need to communicate. But how he makes his *letters* does not (the college professor or senator could have terrible handwriting). The situation in China, on the other hand, is just the opposite. How a person makes his characters has importance far beyond his need to communicate, but how he makes his sounds does not. In England the educated community is distinguished by and held together by the way its members talk; and they wear their accent like a badge of membership. But in China the educated community throughout history has always been held together by writing—not speaking—and the badge of membership had to lie in the writing. Today, the members of the educated community all learn P̆utōnghuà (common spoken Chinese), but the badge hasn't changed. And the only strong incentive to approach the Peking standard of pronunciation is to come just close enough to communicate. There is little reward for coming any closer: they already have their badge. It is quite normal for very important people to talk in the equivalent of Cockney or Brooklynese (as did Mao Tsetung).

So even though Putonghua has the pronunciation of Peking as its standard and has been popularized through the schools and media, what you should, in fact, be prepared to hear is many different varieties of Putonghua, depending on where each speaker comes from: 'Shandong Putonghua' (a dialect of Northern Mandarin), 'Shanghai Putonghua' (Putonghua that has been learned with a Shanghai accent), etc. Here are some of the commonest departures from 'Peking Putonghua' you will encounter.

1. The dropping of the 'retroflex h': zh > z, ch > c, sh > s.
2. The combining of final nasals: -n > -ng or -ng > -n.
3. The nasalization of vowels in place of final nasals:
   an > ã, ang > ã, etc.
4. The confusion of initial n and l: n > l.

And the tonal departures will often not even appear to follow rules. The best advice to the student is to strive to come as close to the Peking standard as possible, while learning to understand the endless varieties.

LESSON 20

SEEING SOMEONE OFF

送 別

A. Dialog: Pinyin Transcription

Ānnā: Àiméi, nǐ zǎo a, zhēn bugǎndāng,[1]   1

            nǐmen hái lái sòng wǒmen.   2

Àiméi: Ài,[*] wǒmen yīnggāi[2] lái sòngsong nǐmen de.   3

            Dōngxi dōu shōushi hǎole ma?   4

Ānnā: Hǎole.   5

Wáng: Nā wǒmen shàng qìchē qù fēijī chǎng ba.   6

Zhòng: Hǎo. Zǒu ba.   7

            (Zài fēijī chǎng.)   8

Tāngmǔ: Chàbuduō gāi shàng fēijī le ba.[3]   9

Àiméi: Duì, chàbuduō le.   10

            Nǐmen dàole jiā jiù gěi wǒmen xiě xìn, á!   11

Tāngmǔ: Yídìng yidìng.   12

Àiméi: Zhù nǐmen yīlù píng ān.[4]   13

Wáng: Yīlù shùn fēng.[5]   14

Tāngmǔ, Ānnā: Zài jiàn, zài ··· jiàn ···   15

[*] Falling-rising-falling intonation (see page 172).

B. Dialog: Simplified Characters

安娜: 爱梅，你早啊，真不敢当[1]，
你们还来送我们。

爱梅: 嗳，我们应该[2]来送送你们的。
东西都收拾好了吗？

安娜: 好了。

王: 那我们上汽车去飞机场吧。

众: 好。走吧。

(在飞机场)

汤姆: 差不多该上飞机了吧[3]。

爱梅: 对，差不多了。
你们到了家就给我们写仗，啊！

汤姆: 一定一定。

爱梅: 祝你们一路平安[4]。

王: 一路顺风[5]。

汤姆}
安娜}: 再见，再一见一。

C. Dialog: Yale Transcription

Ānnā: Àiméi, nǐ dzǎu a, jēn bugǎndāng,[1]   1

           nǐmen hái lái sùng wǒmen.   2

Àiméi: Ǎi,* wǒmen yīnggāi[2] lái sùngsung nǐmen de.   3

           Dūngsyi dōu shōushr hǎule ma?   4

Ānnā: Hǎule.   5

Wáng: Nà wǒmen shàng chìchē chyù fēijī chǎng ba.   6

Jùng: Hǎu. Dzǒu ba.   7

           (Dzài fēijī chǎng.)   8

Tāngmǔ: Chàbudwō gāi shàng fēijī le ba.[3]   9

Àiméi: Dwèi, chàbudwō le.   10

           Nǐmen dàule jyā jyòu gěi wǒmen syě syìn, á!   11

Tāngmǔ: Yídìng yidìng.   12

Àiméi: Jù nǐmen yīlù píng ān.[4]   13

Wáng: Yīlù shwùn fēng.[5]   14

Tāngmǔ, Ānnā: Dzài jyàn, dzài ··· jiàn ···   15

* Falling-rising-falling intonation (see page 172).

D. DIALOG: FULL CHARACTERS

安娜：愛梅，你早啊，真不敢當[1]，   1
　　　你們還來送我們。   2

愛梅：噯，我們應該[2]來送送你們的。   3
　　　東西都收拾好了嗎？   4

安娜：好了。   5

王：　那我們上汽車去飛機場吧。   6

眾：　好。走吧。   7

　　　（在飛機場）   8

湯姆：差不多該上飛機了吧[3]。   9

愛梅：對，差不多了。   10
　　　你們到了家就給我們寫信，啊！   11

湯姆：一定一定。   12

愛梅：祝你們一路平安[4]。   13

王：　一路順風[5]。   14

湯姆
安娜 ｝：再見，再一見一。   15

E. Dialog: Vocabulary and Notes

别
bié
To leave, to part.

飞机场
fēijī chǎng
Airport.

敢当
gǎndāng
To dare to do.

平安
píng ān
Safe, secure; peaceful.

应该
yīnggāi
Should, ought to.

写仪
xiě xìn
To write a letter.

收拾
shōu•shí
To put in order.

顺
shùn
In the same direction.

上汽车
shàng qìchē
To get in a car.

顺风
shùn fēng
Go with the wind.

1. <u>bugǎndāng</u>.[a] I'm not worthy of what you've done for me.

2. <u>yīnggāi</u>.[b] This may sound a little ungracious in English (where one should say 'want to', not 'should'), but it is the proper thing to say in Chinese.

3. <u>chàbuduō gāi</u> ...[c]. 'Almost should'; that is, 'almost time to'.

4. <u>yīlù píng ān</u>.[d] (I wish you) one road of (that is, one trip full of) peace and safety.

5. <u>yīlù shùn fēng</u>.[e] (I wish you) a whole trip with the wind at your back. 'May the wind be with you' is something like 'May God be with you.'

a. 不敢当   c. 差不多该···   d. 一路平安

b. 应该   e. 一路顺风

F. Dialog: English

Anna: Good morning, Aimei. We're unworthy of this ···   1

         your coming to see us off.   2

Aimei: Oh, it's only right that we should see you off.   3

         Is everything packed and ready to go?   4

Anna: All ready.   5

Wang: Well, into the car and off to the airport, then.   6

All: Yes, let's go.   7

         (At the airport.)   8

Tom: It's almost time to board the plane.   9

Aimer: Yes, almost.   10

         Write us when you get home, you hear?   11

Tom: We will, without fail.   12

Aimei: I hope you have a safe journey.   13

Wang: And may the wind stay at your back all the way.   14

Tom and Anna: Goodbye. Good ··· bye ··· .   15

G. SUBSTITUTIONS: FULL CHARACTERS AND ENGLISH

1. 差不多該上飛機了吧。
   吃飯
   走
   上學
   下課
   放學

   It's almost time to board the plane.
                   to eat
                   to go
                   to go to class
                   for class to finish
                   to go home from school

2. 我們上出租汽車　去　飛機場。
   上飛機　　　　　舊金山
   下輪船　　　　　上海
   上火車　　　　　北京

   我們上公共汽車就到　家

   We took a taxi   to the airport.
           plane   to San Francisco
           ship   to Shanghai
           train   to Peking
           bus   home

H. SUBSTITUTIONS: SIMPLIFIED CHARACTERS AND PINYIN

差不多该上飞机了吧。
      吃饭
      走
      上学
      下课
      放学

1.

Chàbuduō gāi shàng fēijī le ba.
      chī fàn
      zǒu
      shàng xué
      xià kè
      fàng xué

2.

我们上出租汽车   去   飞机场。
    上飞机   旧金山
    下轮船   上海
    上火车   北京
我们上公共汽车   就到   家。

Wǒmen shàng chūzū qìchē   qù   fēijī chǎng
      shàng fēijī   Jiùjīnshān
      xià lúnchuán   Shànghǎi
      shàng huǒchē   Běijīng
Wǒmen shàng gōnggòng qìchē jiù dào jiā.

I. Mini Dialogs: Full Characters and English

1.
A. 這一年，我們兩個成了最知己的朋友了。
　B. 你走了，我會想死你的，唉！
A. 別難過，我給你寫信。
　B. 你幾天給我寫一封信呢？
A. 一天一封。

A. We've become such close friends during this past year.
　B. I'll just die without you, (sob).
A. Don't feel so bad; I'll write you.
　B. How often?
A. Every day.

2.
A. 啊呀，時間到了。走了、走了。
　B. 我去送送你。
A. 不用了。
　B. 好。小心慢走。
　　有空再來啊。

A. Oh oh, it's time to go. See you.
　B. I'll see you out.
A. That won't be necessary.
　B. O.K. Drive carefully! (Be careful, go slowly.)
　　Come again when you get a chance.

知己	zhīyǐ Close, intimate.	想死	xiǎng sǐ (nǐ) 'Miss (you) to death.'
封	fēng Classifier for letters.	小心	xiǎoxīn Be careful.

J. MINI DIALOGS: SIMPLIFIED CHARACTERS AND PINYIN

1.
> A. 这一年，我们两个成了最知己的朋友了．
>
> B. 你走了，我会想死你的，唉！
>
> A. 别难过，我给你写伩。
>
> B. 你几天给我写一封伩呢？
>
> A. 一天一封。
>
>
> A. Zhèi yinián women liǎngge chéngle zuì zhīyǐde péngyou le.
> B. Nǐ zǒule, wǒ huì xiǎng sǐ nǐ de. Haih.
> A. Bié nánguò, wǒ gěi nǐ xiě xìn.
> B. Nǐ jǐ tiān gěi xiě yifēng xìn ne?
> A. Yī tiān yī fēng.

2.
> A. 啊呀，时间到了。走了、走了。
>
> B. 我去送送你。
>
> A. 不用了。
>
> B. 好．小心慢走。
>
>   有空再来啊。
>
>
> A. Āyà, shíjiān dàole. Zǒule, zǒule.
> B. Wǒ qù sòngsong nǐ.
> A. Buyòngle.
> B. Hǎo. Xiǎoxīn, màn zǒu.
>   Yǒu kòng zài lái a.

会	huì Will.	难过	nánguò Feel bad or miserable.
慢走	màn zǒu Go slowly (carefully).		

I (2)

3.
A. 我要走了。
B. 忙甚麼呀？吃了飯再走吧。
A. 好吧。

A. I've got to go.
  B. What's the hurry? Eat first.
A. All right.

4.
A. 你一個人出國。
  路上多加小心，啊！
B. 欸。媽，您自己也多保重身體啊！

A. You're going abroad all by yourself.
   Be very careful wherever you go, you hear?
B. I will, Mom. And you take good care of yourself, too.

5.
A. 祝你一路平安。
  B. 寫信，再見，一路順風。
    C. 再見，再見。

A. Have a safe journey!
  B. Be sure to write. Goodbye. May God be with you.
    C. Goodbye! Goodbye!

出國 chū guó
     To go abroad.

加 jiā
   To add or increase

J (2)

3.
> A. 我要走了。
>
> B. 忙什么呀？吃了饭再走吧。
>
> A. 好吧。
>
> A. Wǒ yào zǒule.
> B. Máng shémme ya? Chīle fàn zài zǒu ba.
> A. Hǎo ba.

4.
> A. 你一个人出国。
>
> 路上多加小心，啊！
>
> B. 欸。妈，您自己也多保重身体啊！
>
> A. Nǐ yíge rén chū guó.
> Lùshàng duō jiā xiǎoxīn, á!
> B. Èi. Mā, nín zìjǐ yě duō bǎozhòng shēnti a!

5.
> A. 祝你一路平安。
>
> B. 写仪，再见，一路顺风。
>
> C. 再见，再见。
>
> A. Zhù nǐ yílù píng ān.
> B. Xiěxīn, zài jiàn, yílù shùn fēng.
> C. Zài jiàn, zài jiàn.

保重   bǎozhòng
        Take care of yourself!

K. Cultural Notes

Hugging and Kissing. In most Western cultures, hugging and kissing serve two quite different functions: affectionate greetings and leave-takings, and sexual play. The use of the first function in public is completely acceptable. The use of the second, though sometimes seen, is quite a different matter. The Chinese, though aware of Western customs in this respect, do not themselves make the distinction. That is, they view any kind of hugging and kissing in public in the same way as Westerners view the second function.

This might be made clearer by comparing the following three actions. 1) A goodbye handshake. 2) A goodbye kiss between husband and wife. 3) A kiss used in sexual play. The Westerner will associate 1 and 2 (they serve the same *function*). The Chinese will associate 2 and 3 (they have the same *form*). The Chinese, when seeing a husband kiss his wife goodbye at the airport, might thus wonder why they didn't do this at home before they came to the airport. But to the Westerner this would be like waving goodbye that morning in bed instead of during the plane's takeoff.

Until quite recently hugging and kissing in public by the Chinese was almost never seen. But this is beginning to change. It is now sometimes seen in Chinese movies (much to the discomfort of some members of the audience). And it can also be seen in the parks, where young lovers sometimes go a little beyond the traditional 'love talk' (<u>tán liàn ài</u>[a]).

a. 谈恋爱

GLOSSARY

All words used in this book that are thought to be new for second-year students are listed below alphabetically in pinyin.* The page number for the word's first occurrence in the book is given instead of an English translation. The page number refers to the page where the word is listed as a vocabulary item (section E for the main dialogs, and the bottom of the page for the mini dialogs and a few substitution drills). For words that appear in most substitution drills, the right-hand page number is given (that is, the page that gives the pinyin transcription). If a new word in a substitution drill later appears in a dialog, it is listed as a vocabulary item for that dialog—and this is the page that is referred to in the glossary, even though the word first appeared in a substitution drill. The reason for this is that most new words in substitution drills are simply for exposure and reference—not memory.

* The ordering is not *completely* by pinyin. All expressions with the same first *character* are grouped together, and characters with the same pinyin are ordered by number of strokes.

ài rén 6 爱人

ānpái 206 安排

Àodàlìyǎ 25 澳大利亚

Bālí 25 巴黎

bá 108 拔

bàba 181 爸爸

bǎihuò shāngdiàn 198 百货商店

bān 241 搬

bàn 252 办

bàngōngshì 38 办公室

bànlù 54 半路

bāng 70 帮

bāngmáng 70 帮忙

bǎo 146 饱

bǎozhòng 301 保重

běi bù 270 北部

bèi 105 背

béng 54 甭

bí 102 鼻

bí•tì 102 鼻涕

bǐrú 178 比如

biàn chéng 229 变成

biàn fàn 146 便饭

biàn 258 遍

biǎo•shì 206 表示

bié 14, 294 别

bié rén 6 别人

bīngqílín 151 冰淇淋

bìng 102 病

bō 38 拨

bó•shì 13 博士

dān•wù 54 耽误
dàngāo 206 蛋糕
dāngrán 280 当然
dào qiàn 54 道歉
Déguo 25 德国
déle 22 得了
dēng 220 登
děng 38 等
děng•yú 178 等于
dǐ 165 底
dìdiǎn 206 地点
dì xià 225 地下
dìzhǐ 257 地址
dìdi 9 弟弟
diǎn 154 点
diǎnxīn 149 点心
diǎnzhōng 38 点钟
diànhuà 38 电话
diànlíng 236 电铃
diàntī 241 电梯

diànyā 245 电压
diànyǐng 136 电影
diànyǐng yuàn 259 电影院
diàn 63 惦
dǐng 165 顶
dìng 271 订
dìng fángjiān 236 订房间
dōngběi 269 东北
Dōngjīng 25 东京
dòu•fu 149 豆腐
dú 86 读
dùzi 109 肚子
dù 102 度
duàn 280 段
duàn 45 断
duìle 22 对了
duìyu 266 对于
duìhuàn 185 兑换
duìhuàn chù 185 兑换处
duō 220 多

duō jiǔ 92 多久
è 57 饿
értóng 10 儿童
ér yǔ 181 儿语
érzi 9 儿子
ěr•duo 105 耳朵
Fàguo 25 法国
fàndiàn 136 饭店
fāng•biàn 135 方便
fāngxiàng 252 方向
fángjiān 236 房间
fàng xué 297 放学
fēijī 60 飞机
fēijī chǎng 294 飞机场
fēi 220 非
féizào 195 肥皂
fèiyán 107 肺炎
fēn 178 分
fēnjī 38 分机
fēng 298 封

fēng 54 峰

fú 244 伏

fúwù 236 服务

fúwù tái 236 服务台

fúwù yuán 236 服务员

fúhào 182 符号

fù·qīn 9 父亲

fù qián 153 付钱

gāi 70 该

gǎi 54 改

gānbēi 213 干杯

gān·jìng 244 干净

gǎndāng 294 敢当

gǎnmào 102 感冒

gàn 94 干

gāng 6 刚

gāo gēn xié 229 高跟鞋

gāo·xìng 12 高兴

gēge 9 哥哥

gēr 209 歌儿

gè wèi 213 各位

gěi 228 给

gōngkē 27 工科

gōngzuò 11 工作

gōnggòng qìchē 54 公共汽车

gōng jīn 107 公斤

gōng lǐ 220 公里

gōngyuán 228 公元

gōng·fū 121 功夫

gōngkè 269 功课

gōngdiàn 225 宫殿

gōng·xǐ 210 恭喜

gòng 287 共

gǔdǒng 192 古董

gǔ jì 266 古迹

gùgōng 225 故宫

gù·shì 167 故事

guǎi 252 拐

guàibude 86 怪不得

guān 73 关

guān·xì 54 关系

guānglín 137 光临

guāngmíng 209 光明

Guǎngdōng 25 广东

Guǎngzhōu 25 广州

guì xìng 31 贵姓

guójì 252 国际

guò jǐ tiān 102 过几天

guòjiǎng 86 过奖

guò qù 60 过去

guò shēng·rì 206 过生日

hái 102 还

hái·shì 86 还是

hǎi 223 海

hǎi wèr 155 海味儿

hàipà 108 害怕

hǎo chī 146 好吃